A KEY ᴛᴏ ᴛʜᴇ ᴡᴏᴏᴅᴌᴄᴇ OF BRITAIN AND IRELAND

STEPHEN P. HOPKIN

Department of Pure and Applied Zoology, University of Reading,
PO Box 228, Reading RG6 2AJ

Abstract

A fully-illustrated, AIDGAP-tested key is provided to the 37 species of woodlice (Crustacea: Isopoda, Oniscidea) now known to be native or naturalised in Britain and Ireland. Glasshouse aliens that cannot breed here in the wild have been excluded. Colour plates support detailed line drawings and the confirmatory descriptions of each species include notes on distribution and natural history. Details are given of the Isopod Recording Scheme and it is hoped that this user-friendly key will stimulate more people to identify woodlice, contribute records, and increase our knowledge of these widespread and interesting animals.

Contents

Introduction

Woodlice are among the most familiar of animals. They have featured prominently throughout history in recipes (Holt, 1885, included a recipe for 'woodlouse sauce'), in the poetry of Sir John Betjeman, the novels of Jean Paul Sartre, the paintings of Paul Klee (Chater, 1988) and have even provided the inspiration for a sermon (Thornton, 1989). In the past, woodlice were often carried in a small pouch attached to a cord around the neck. These were swallowed as a cure for stomach aches and other minor ailments. It is possible that the calcium carbonate in their exoskeletons is able to neutralise stomach acids although I confess I have not had the courage to test this theory!

The beneficial effects of woodlice far outweigh any damage that they do. However, woodlice have an ill-deserved reputation as pests, mainly because they wander into houses at night, usually to escape supersaturation with water during wet weather. Woodlice may travel considerable distances during these nocturnal rambles. I have found some specimens trapped inside a light shade of a bedroom on the first floor of a building. In the garden, woodlice rarely attack living plants, preferring to eat v

to decompose. In glasshouses, woodlice may occasionally nibble seedlings but they rarely do any significant economic damage. In the litter layer of deciduous woods, and on compost heaps, woodlice perform a vital role. They chew dead plants into small fragments and deposit these as faecal pellets which decompose rapidly. Woodlice may also graze fungal hyphae from leaves (Gunnarson, 1987) or their own faecal pellets (Hassall and Rushton, 1982; 1985) and this may form an important source of nutrients when the only food available is of poor quality. Deposition of faecal pellets containing fungal spores in deep moist leaf litter by woodlice may be important in stimulating decomposition in woodlands (Hassall *et al.*, 1987). Thus, the feeding activities of woodlice speed up the decomposition process and help to return essential nutrients to the soil.

All British woodlice are predominantly vegetarian. However, there are some foreign species that have a more varied diet. In New Zealand, the main food of the sand beach woodlouse *Scyphax ornatus* is drowned honeybees (Quilter, 1987). In the U.S.A., woodlice are used by museum workers to clean the flesh from delicate vertebrate skeletons (Maiorana and Van Valen, 1985).

Woodlice are members of the class Crustacea, which also includes crabs, shrimps and lobsters. Most crustaceans are aquatic. Only two orders contain species which are able to live their whole life cycle away from water. These are the Isopoda, which includes the woodlice, and the Amphipoda. In the British Isles, only one species of amphipod, *Arcitalitrus dorrieni*, can live permanently on land. This was introduced to Britain from Australia and is now quite widespread in Cornwall and South Devon (Harding and Sutton, 1988). It has been discovered recently in several other areas of Britain including Kew Gardens.

The order Isopoda contains more than 10,000 species worldwide, most of which are marine. About 3,500 species of woodlice (Suborder Oniscidea) have been described but there are probably at least as many waiting to be discovered (Schmalfuss, personal communication), especially in tropical rain forests. Isopods evolved in the sea and are thought to have made the transition to land via the seashore. Species such as the common sea slater, *Ligia oceanica* (PLATE 1A, 1B), are still restricted to the coast. Successive species became increasingly resistant to the rigours of a terrestrial existence and probably colonised the land via moist leaf litter of pteridophytes (horsetails and ferns) during the Carboniferous (Piearce, 1989). Two key features 'pre-adapted' marine isopods to colonise the land. First, the dorso-ventral flattening of the body gave an extremely stable 'squat' posture when walking. Second, retention of the young in a fluid-filled brood pouch protected them from drying out in the first few weeks after hatching from the egg. All isopods have seven pairs of legs which are usually of similar structure (hence the name *iso*-pod from the Greek *isos* meaning 'equal' and *podes* meaning feet).

Traditionally, woodlice have been regarded as poorly adapted to life on land. However, research conducted in recent years has shown that woodlice have evolved several sophisticated physiological and behavioural mechanisms to control water loss. These include the modification of the pleopods to form lungs (PLATE 8B) and a capillary conducting system which allows nitrogenous waste to be excreted as ammonia gas, without significant loss of water (Hoese, 1984). Indeed the Dutch word for woodlice, 'pissebed', is probably derived from the smell of urine that large aggregations of woodlice give off.

Woodlice have colonised some of the most extreme environments on earth including deserts in Israel and North Africa, and hypersaline pools in Australia via fully terrestrial forms (Blinn *et al.*, 1989). The desert species *Hemilepistus reaumuri* occurs in burrows at densities of greater than $100 \, \text{m}^{-2}$ (Hoffmann, 1984). This remarkable woodlouse pairs for life and is able to relocate its burrow using the position of the sun in the sky. The juveniles help to maintain the burrow. Thus, this species is the nearest we have to true social behaviour (eusociality) in woodlice. Individual *Hemilepistus* are able to walk several kilometres in a few days, quite a feat in the rigorous desert environment.

The only animals known to prey exclusively on woodlice are spiders of the genus *Dysdera* (PLATE 11A). Many other animals will, however, eat them and toads can be reared to adulthood on a diet that consists entirely of woodlice. In terms of impact of predation on numbers, centipedes consume about 40% of all woodlice that are eaten. The great majority of woodlice that fall victim to predators are immature (Sunderland and Sutton, 1980).

All woodlice have six pairs of legs when released from the brood pouch of the female. At this stage, they are called mancas. After the first moult, which occurs within 24 hours of release, the 7th leg bearing segment appears and after another moult they gain their full complement of seven pairs of legs and are juveniles. Juveniles moult at regular intervals until they reach sexual maturity, usually within a year, when they become adults. The moulting process continues after maturity (although with less frequency) and involves shedding the exoskeleton in two parts. The posterior part (*pleon* and *pereon* segments 5,6 and 7: see Fig. 2) is shed a few days before the anterior part (*head* and *pereon* segments 1,2,3, and 4). Few woodlice live for more than two or three years. The life cycles of woodlice are quite variable between species, and different geographical areas. The common pill woodlouse, *Armadillidium vulgare*, for example (PLATE 16A), lives for 4 years in California (where it was introduced at the turn of the century) and females have 3 or 4 broods in a lifetime; at Spurn Head in Yorkshire, however, females of the same species have only 2 broods whilst at Lakenheath in Suffolk they have only one (Sutton *et al.*, 1984).

The common striped woodlouse, *Philoscia muscorum* (PLATE 6B), on dune grassland exhibits a clear example of 'year class splitting'. Individuals born in one season differentiate into two forms, one of which grows to maturity in one year, the other in two (Grundy and Sutton, 1989). Such flexibility is one of the reasons why woodlice are so successful in colonising disturbed environments.

Only 37 species of woodlice are known to breed out of doors in the British Isles (another ten or so have been recorded only in glasshouses). They range from 2 mm to 30 mm in length. Two species, *Oniscus asellus* (PLATES 6A, 7A) and *Porcellio scaber* (PLATE 11A), are particularly common around buildings and are ideal animals with which to conduct simple laboratory experiments (a range of which were described by Sutton, 1972). There is even one species, *Platyarthrus hoffmannseggi* (PLATE 5B), which is always found associated with ants.

Earlier keys to British woodlice have proved difficult for the beginner to use. Edney's (1954) Synopsis was a specialist's key which relied at many points on characters which were difficult to see with a hand lens, or required dissection. Also, some of the features that were used are not visible in specimens preserved in 70% alcohol. Sutton, Harding and Burn's key (included in Sutton, 1972) contained a number of clear and accurate line drawings, together with a series of beautiful colour paintings of a selection of species. This key was easier to use as it relied, as far as possible, on characters which could be seen with the naked eye, or a hand lens. Publication of Sutton, Harding and Burn's key stimulated an upsurge in interest in woodlice. There is now a need for a new key which incorporates up-to-date information on distribution and descriptions of the seven species discovered in Britain since 1972.

Recent discoveries on parasites (Colloff and Hopkin, 1986; 1987), the structure and function of the digestive system (Hames and Hopkin, 1989) and the accumulation of metal pollutants by woodlice (Hopkin, 1989a; Hopkin *et al.*, 1986) have shown that there is much that remains to be discovered about the biology and distribution of these fascinating and, dare I say it, endearing creatures. It is hoped that publication of this key will encourage further interest in 'grammerzows', 'chiggy pigs' and 'cheeselogs'!

COLLECTION AND PRESERVATION OF WOODLICE

Woodlice occur in a wide range of habitats and can be searched for almost anywhere. The most productive sites are those which provide numerous crevices and microsites where the woodlice can hide. Thus, damp leaf litter, rotting wood, loose bark, piles of rocks in disused quarries, and 'mature' tips of household refuse and rubble are 'good' sites. Six species of woodlice are found only on the coast (under boulders, in rock crevices and under driftwood) and are much easier to find at night (with a torch) when they come out to feed (see Checklist p. 604). Harding and Sutton (1985) provide a detailed analysis of habitat preferences of British woodlice based on the results of the Isopod Survey Scheme.

Hand-searching among surface material ('grubbing about'), or even direct observation, will turn up many of the larger species of woodlice. In a Bristol garden, for example, I have observed large numbers of *Armadillidium depressum* (PLATE 15) walking over a brick wall in full sunlight on a hot July day with no apparent distress. However, some species are vulnerable to drying out, particularly the small soil-dwelling forms. These can be found only by digging into the soil, or by turning over deeply-embedded boulders. Remember to look very closely on the underside of such stones and in the cavities from which the boulders were dislodged (and to put the rocks back when you have finished!). Pitfall traps may be useful for sampling in areas from which it would otherwise be difficult to collect (*e.g.* shingle beaches) and sieving humus onto a tray may turn up some of the more inconspicuous soil species. Sutton (1972) and Chalmers and Parker (1989) contain detailed discussions of collection methods and techniques.

For the beginner, a hand lens of at least 10 × magnification is essential for the identification of specimens in the field. With experience, it is possible to recognise most of the larger species with the naked eye. Other useful equipment includes a strong penknife for levering bark from rotting wood (try not to remove more than 10% of this from each log) and a pair of weak 'storksbill' forceps. Smaller species can be picked up with a moistened paintbrush.

Identification of larger species of woodlice can be attempted with live specimens in the field by holding them between the first finger and thumb (PLATE 8A) (woodlice do not bite or sting!), or restraining specimens in a suitable holding and viewing device (see Jones-Walters, 1989, for examples). The smaller 'pygmy' woodlice (Family Trichoniscidae) are more delicate and can be examined with a hand lens while still attached to a piece of substratum such as a small lump of soil or fragment of bark. Most species will survive for several days in self-seal polythene bags on which site details can be written with an indelible pen. Some leaf litter, or moss, from the collection site should be included and the bags should be kept cool and away from direct sunlight. Tiny specimens are best placed individually in small glass or plastic tubes with tightly fitting lids. Using such methods, live woodlice are safely transported back to the laboratory/classroom for more detailed observation. Alternatively, woodlice can be placed directly in preservative in the field. However,

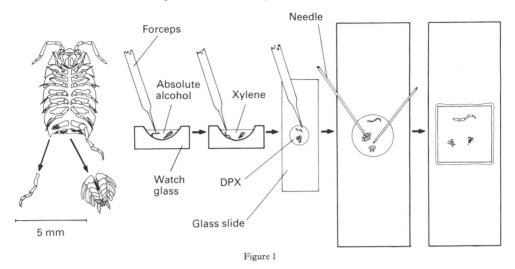

Figure 1

Schematic diagram showing the procedure for permanent mounting of legs and pleopods on a microscope slide. After preservation of the whole woodlouse in 70% alcohol for at least 24 hrs, the leg and pleon are removed and dehydrated in absolute alcohol for at least one hour, cleared in xylene for 30 minutes and placed on a slide in a drop of DPX. The first and second pleopods can then be teased away from the pleon with a pair of mounted needles and the specimen spread out under a cover slip.

by doing this, many characters which are extremely helpful in identification (some colours, number of lungs, behaviour etc.) will be lost.

Woodlice cannot be set and pinned in the same way as insects. Because their cuticle is heavily calcified, woodlice become very brittle when dry. Therefore, they must be immersed permanently in a preservative such as 70% alcohol (*i.e.* 3 parts water to 7 parts alcohol or clear industrial methylated spirit). Specimens are kept ideally in glass tubes with tightly-fitting plastic tops. It is essential to include a label (inside the tube) on which is written, in pencil or indelible ink, the Name of the species, the Collector (even if it is you), the Locality, the Ordnance Survey Grid Reference and the Date on which the specimen was collected. Remember, someone may want to consult your specimen in 100 years time; accurate labels are very important.

Positive identification of a few of the small species of woodlice may require removal and examination of the pleopods and 7th legs of a male. An example of a typical method for making permanent slide mounts of such material is shown in Fig. 1. Xylene and DPX must be used in a fume cupboard and there are restrictions on their use in schools. Less toxic alternatives may be available and it is best to check with biological suppliers as to current recommended chemicals since new products appear on the market all the time.

WOODLICE CULTURES

Some people may not regard woodlice as the most stimulating of pets, but most species breed readily in captivity and make an interesting addition to a classroom or laboratory display. Ideal containers are clear plastic sandwich boxes containing a thin layer of soil, a few pieces of bark and some leaf litter. The addition of a few shreds of grated carrot every week, and a light spray with water, will keep the cultures healthy. Care should be taken not to make conditions too damp since woodlice are just as easily killed by conditions being too moist as being too dry.

THE ISOPOD RECORDING SCHEME

In common with many other groups of animals, an active recording scheme exists for woodlice in Britain. This is co-ordinated by the Biological Records Centre (BRC) of the Natural Environment Research Council's Institute of Terrestrial Ecology at Monks Wood Experimental Station. The Isopod Survey Scheme was established in 1968 and, to date, more than 30,000 individual species records have been submitted. Harding and Sutton (1985) give a detailed account of the development of the Isopod Survey Scheme, together with habitat information and distribution maps for records received until August 1982. These maps still provide an accurate picture of the general distribution of most woodlice in Britain and Ireland. However, the known ranges of some species have been extended since 1982, probably as a result of increased collecting rather than a true ecological expansion. Maps of 14 species, including records to 1987, have been published by Hopkin (1987), and more detailed surveys of local areas have been reported for Reading (Hopkin, 1988), Cornwall (Jones, 1987) and the Isles of Scilly (Jones and Pratley, 1987). Maps of the distributions of *Trachelipus rathkei* and *Armadillidium pictum*, which include records subsequent to Harding and Sutton (1985), have also appeared recently (Whitehead, 1988; Richardson, 1989). The notes on distribution in the individual descriptions of species, included here after the key, give up-to-date information based on records received to August 1991.

New recorders are welcome to join the Isopod Survey Scheme which currently has about 150 members. Those registered receive a newsletter twice a year and are encouraged to participate in the annual field meeting held jointly with the British Myriapod Group. A journal 'Isopoda' is also published which contains a variety of articles on terrestrial and freshwater isopods and amphipods. Write in the first instance to BRC (address below) who will forward your enquiry to the current scheme organiser.

Isopod Survey Scheme, Biological Records Centre, Monks Wood Experimental Station, Abbots Ripton, Huntingdon, Cambs PE17 2LS.

SYSTEMATIC CHECKLIST

This checklist gives the names which are currently accepted for the 37 species of woodlice known to be native or naturalised to Britain and Ireland. The list is based on that given by Harding and Sutton (1985), with the addition of three species (*Haplophthalmus montivagus*, *Metatrichoniscoides leydigi* and *Trichoniscoides helveticus*) which have been discovered in Britain since 1985. The names given to *Stenophiloscia zosterae*, *Porcellionides cingendus* and *Porcellionides pruinosus* have been adopted relatively recently. The previous names for these species are given in brackets under the current names opposite. At least ten other species have been recorded from glasshouses at some time during the last 100 years. However, these are not included in either the checklist or the key since there is no evidence that they can breed here in the wild. Also, identification of these species is very difficult as several have yet to be discovered in the countries from which they were transported, presumably in potted plants. Details of these 'alien' species, and a comprehensive list of synonyms of British woodlice, are given by Harding and Sutton (1985).

I have suggested vernacular names for the eight most common and widespread species. These are remembered more easily by children, who can graduate subsequently to the scientific names. These differ from the common names suggested by Seymour (1989) which are, in my opinion, quite difficult to remember and in some cases are misleading. Also included on the list are the type of antennal flagellum and number of pairs of pleopodal lungs (if present) in each species. This information can be cross-referenced with the key.

CLASSIFICATION LIST

PLEOPODAL LUNGS	CLASS CRUSTACEA Order Isopoda Suborder Oniscidea	ANTENNAL FLAGELLUM
None	**Family Ligiidae** *Ligia oceanica* (Linnaeus, 1767)—Plate 1A, 1B (Common sea slater) *Ligidium hypnorum* (Cuvier, 1792)	10 or more distinct sections (Fig. 5a)
	Family Trichoniscidae *Androniscus dentiger* Verhoeff, 1908—Plate 3B (Rosy woodlouse) *Buddelundiella cataractae* Verhoeff, 1930 *Haplophthalmus danicus* Budde-Lund, 1880 *Haplophthalmus mengei* (Zaddach, 1844)—Plate 2B *Haplophthalmus montivagus* Verhoeff, 1941—Plate 2A *Metatrichoniscoides celticus* Oliver & Trew, 1981 *Metatrichoniscoides leydigi* (Weber, 1880)—Plate 2B *Miktoniscus patiencei* Vandel, 1946 *Oritoniscus flavus* (Budde-Lund, 1906)—Plate 3A *Trichoniscoides albidus* (Budde-Lund, 1880)—Plate 5A *Trichoniscoides helveticus* (Carl, 1908) *Trichoniscoides saeroeensis* Lohmander, 1923 *Trichoniscoides sarsi* Patience, 1908 *Trichoniscus pusillus* Brandt, 1833—Plate 4A, 4B (Common pygmy woodlouse) *Trichoniscus pygmaeus* Sars, 1899	One distinct conical section that tapers to a point (Fig. 5d)
	Family Halophilosciidae *Halophiloscia couchi* (Kinahan, 1858)—Plate 7B *Stenophiloscia zosterae* Verhoeff, 1928 (= *Halophiloscia zosterae*) **Family Oniscidae** *Oniscus asellus* Linnaeus, 1758—Plate 6A, 7A (Common shiny woodlouse) **Family Philosciidae** *Philoscia muscorum* (Scopoli, 1763)—Plate 6 (Common striped woodlouse)	Three distinct sections (Fig. 5b)
Two pairs (e.g. Fig. 3)	**Family Platyarthridae** *Platyarthrus hoffmannseggi* Brandt, 1833—Plate 5B (Ant woodlouse) **Family Porcellionidae** *Porcellio dilatatus* Brandt 1833—Plate 10A, 10B *Porcellio laevis* Latreille, 1804—Plate 9A *Porcellio scaber* Latreille, 1804—Plate 6, 11A (Common rough woodlouse) *Porcellio spinicornis* Say, 1818—Plate 9B *Porcellionides cingendus* (Kinahan, 1857)—Plate 12A (= *Metoponorthus cingendus*) *Porcellionides pruinosus* (Brandt, 1833)—Plate 12B (= *Metoponorthus pruinosus*) **Family Armadillidiidae** *Armadillidium album* Dollfus, 1877—Plate 13B *Armadillidium depressum* Brandt, 1833—Plate 15A, 15B *Armadillidium nasatum* Budde-Lund, 1885 *Armadillidium pictum* Brandt, 1833—Plate 14B *Armadillidium pulchellum* (Zenker, 1798)—Plate 14A *Armadillidium vulgare* (Latreille, 1804)—Plate 16A, 16B (Common pill woodlouse) *Eluma purpurascens* Budde-Lund, 1885—Plate 13A	Two distinct sections (Fig. 5c)
Five pairs (e.g. Plate 8B)	**Family Cylisticidae** *Cylisticus convexus* (De Geer, 1778)—Plate 8A, 8B **Family Trachelipidae** *Trachelipus rathkei* (Brandt, 1833)—Plate 11B	

*Restricted to coastal sites

INTRODUCTION TO THE KEY

The key is designed to enable all woodlice in Britain and Ireland to be identified to species. All the figures have been drawn with reference to preserved and, in most cases (*Stenophiloscia zosterae* and *Metatrichoniscoides celticus* excluded), live British and/or Irish specimens. The colour plates are of live unrestrained woodlice in the field or laboratory. Photographs were taken on Ektachrome (100 transparency film with an Olympus OM4 camera, zoom extension tubes, 38 mm and 80 mm macro lenses and a flashgun mounted on the front of the lens. The most important diagnostic features used are those which can still be seen clearly in specimens which have been in 70% alcohol for at least 24 hours. Often, these features are complemented by additional characters which are visible in live specimens. These include colour (which may fade in alcohol), the number of pairs of lungs (which is not visible in preserved woodlice) and behaviour (can the animal roll into a ball? how fast does it run? etc.).

The majority of adult and juvenile woodlice will key out to species with the aid of a 10 × hand lens. However, a dissecting microscope with a strong overhead light source will make the task much easier. Such equipment is particularly useful for determining the number of ocelli in the eyes of the small soil-dwelling 'pygmy' woodlice in the Family Trichoniscidae. In a small number of cases, the pleopods and/or 7th legs of males may have to be examined for positive identification (see Fig. 3). However, the species involved are scarce and are unlikely to be encountered by the beginner.

All juvenile and adult woodlice have seven pairs of legs and this should prevent confusion with any other group of terrestrial arthropods (Tilling, 1987). The pill millipede, *Glomeris marginata*, is sometimes mistaken for a pill woodlouse (*Armadillidium* spp.), but *Glomeris* has many more legs (17 or 19 pairs in the adult) and fewer segments at the posterior end (PLATE 16A).

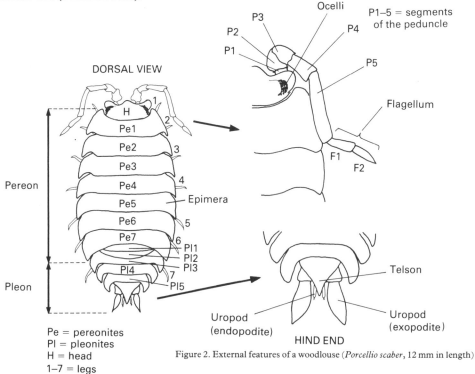

Figure 2. External features of a woodlouse (*Porcellio scaber*, 12 mm in length)

Pe = pereonites
Pl = pleonites
H = head
1–7 = legs

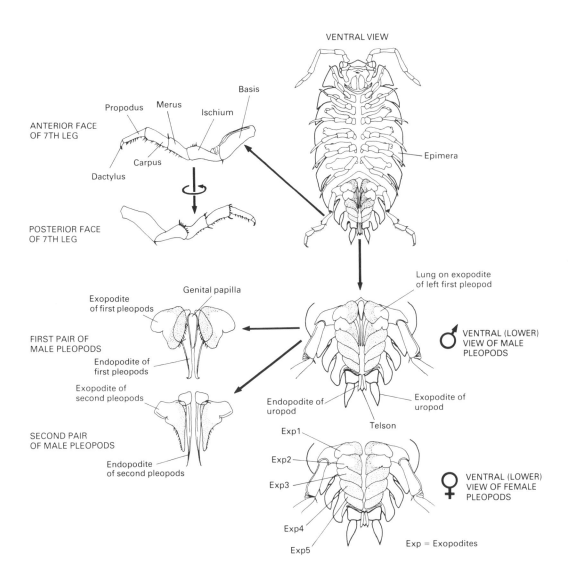

Figure 3. External features of a woodlouse (*Porcellio scaber*, of 12 mm length)

THE KEY

If you have never attempted to identify a woodlouse before, it is a good idea to practice using the key with some specimens collected from your garden, school etc. Four species are widespread and common throughout Britain and Ireland. These are the common shiny woodlouse, *Oniscus asellus* (PLATE 6A, 7A), the common rough woodlouse, *Porcellio scaber* (PLATE 11A), the common striped woodlouse, *Philoscia muscorum* (PLATE 6B), and the common pygmy woodlouse, *Trichoniscus pusillus* (PLATE 4A, 4B). A fifth species, the common pill woodlouse, *Armadillidium vulgare* (PLATE 16A, 16B), is widespread in Wales, southern England and southern Ireland, but to the north of these areas it tends to be restricted to the coast. These five common species are known amongst isopodologists as the 'big five' or 'famous five'. They are asterisked in the key.

Start at couplet 1 in the key. This is a true dichotomous key—all levels provide a couplet with two alternatives. Check your specimen carefully against the character(s) listed before deciding which route to take. If you get stuck and your specimen does not appear to fit either alternative, work back to the previous couplet and take a closer look. If you come across a word which you do not understand, consult Figs. 2 and 3 and/ or the Glossary (page 648). Comprehensive descriptions of each species are given in a separate section immediately after the key. Figures 2 and 3 are included on pages 606 and 607 and are repeated on the inside back cover.

1a   Uropods much longer than wide, long and tapering to a point (Fig. 4c), or 'spear-shaped' (Fig. 4b) 2

1b   Uropods about as long as wide, flattened and 'spade-like' (Fig. 4a; PLATE 14B) 31

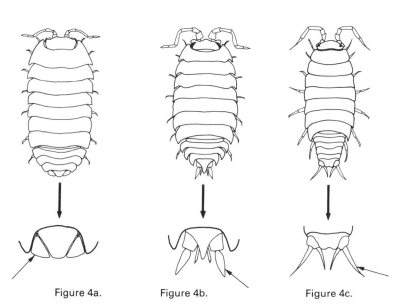

Figure 4a.   Figure 4b.   Figure 4c.

2a (1a) Flagella of antennae with one distinct section tapering to a point (Fig. 5d) or two (Fig. 5c) or three (Fig. 5b) distinct sections; eyes small, composed of a maximum of about 30 ocelli which never cover more than half of the sides of the head (PLATE 7A) 3

2b Flagella of antennae with 10 or more distinct sections; eyes huge, composed of 100 or more ocelli which cover the whole of the side of the head (Fig. 5a; PLATE 1B) 5

Figure 5a.

Flagellum

3a (2a) Flagella of antennae with two (Fig. 5c), or three (Fig. 5b) distinct sections; some species up to 20 mm in length 4

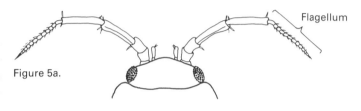

Flagellum

Figure 5b.

3b Flagella of antennae with one distinct conical section which tapers to a point (Fig. 5d) although under high magnification, up to six indistinct sections may be faintly visible (see note under couplet 6 below); maximum length of adults 6 mm (except for *Oritoniscus flavus* (PLATE 3A) which is up to 9 mm but is found only in south-east Ireland) . 6

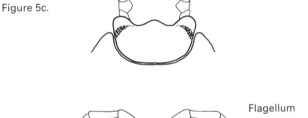

Flagellum

Figure 5c.

Flagellum

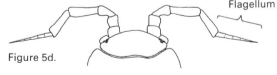

Figure 5d.

4a (3a) Flagella of antennae with three distinct sections (Fig. 5b; PLATE 7A) . . . 20

4b Flagella of antennae with two distinct sections (Fig. 5c; PLATE 9B) . . . 23

5a All four articles of uropods
(2b) of equal length (Fig. 6a);
outline of *pereon* and *pleon* a
smooth line (Fig. 6a; inset);
maximum length 30 mm;
seashore only; common
around entire coast of
Britain and Ireland . .
Ligia oceanica (p. 635)
(PLATE 1A, 1B)

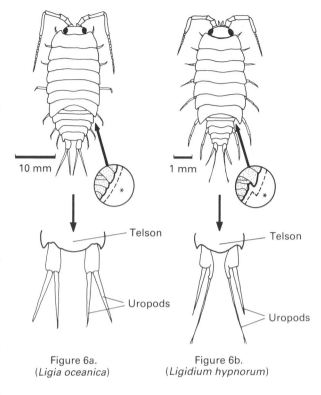

10 mm   1 mm

Telson   Telson

Uropods   Uropods

Figure 6a.   Figure 6b.
(*Ligia oceanica*)   (*Ligidium hypnorum*)

5b Inner two articles of uropods longer than outer two
(Fig. 6b); outline of edges of
pereon and *pleon* a stepped
line (Fig. 6b; inset); maximum length 9 mm; inland
and coastal sites but restricted to the Midlands and
south and east England . .
Ligidium hypnorum
(p. 636)

6(3b) Woodlice having an antennal flagellum with one distinct section that tapers to a point
(Fig. 5d) are the so-called 'pygmy woodlice' (Family Trichoniscidae). The flagellum
is actually composed of six sections but these are fused together and are difficult to
resolve except under high magnification. The pointed tip of the flagellum is made up
of a number of sensory bristles which may separate to form a 'tuft' in preserved
specimens. The majority of the pygmy woodlice are small soil-dwelling forms. Indeed, with the exception of *Oritoniscus flavus* (PLATE 3A) (which is only found in
south east Ireland and reaches 9 mm in length), all species in this group are never
longer than 6 mm. The common pygmy woodlouse, *Trichoniscus pusillus* (PLATE
4A, 4B), and the rosy woodlouse *Androniscus dentiger* (PLATE 3B) are the two
species most likely to be found by beginners. Other smaller species are difficult to
identify with certainty unless a dissecting microscope is used. With some species,
examination of the pleopods and/or 7th legs of males is the only certain method of
identification. Indeed, *Haplophthalmus montivagus* and *Trichoniscoides helveticus*
were discovered in reference collections of *Haplophthalmus mengei* and *Trichoniscoides
sarsi* while drawings were being prepared for this key. Pygmy woodlice should be
examined live, at first if possible, and then preserved in 70% alcohol for more
detailed study with a binocular microscope.

6a   Dorsal surface with pronounced longitudinal ridges (Fig. 7a, 7b); maximum length
     4 mm 7

6b   Dorsal surface smooth (Fig. 7c, 7e), or with transverse rows of small bumps or spines
     (Fig. 7d, 7f, 7g); one species up to 9 mm in length 10

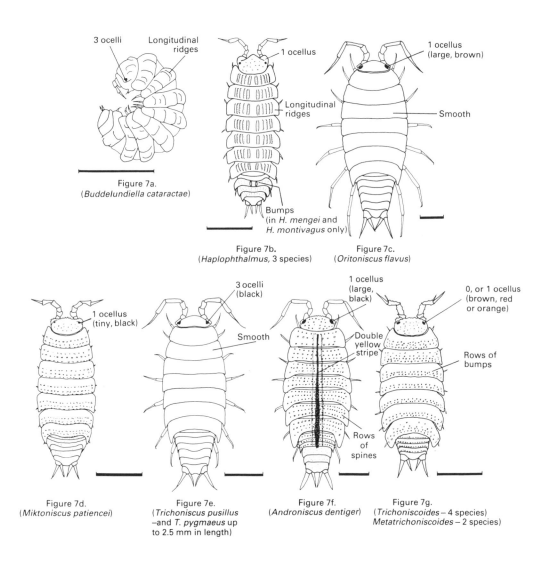

Figure 7a.
(*Buddelundiella cataractae*)

Figure 7b.
(*Haplophthalmus*, 3 species)

Figure 7c.
(*Oritoniscus flavus*)

Figure 7d.
(*Miktoniscus patiencei*)

Figure 7e.
(*Trichoniscus pusillus*
–and *T. pygmaeus* up
to 2.5 mm in length)

Figure 7f.
(*Androniscus dentiger*)

Figure 7g.
(*Trichoniscoides* – 4 species)
(*Metatrichoniscoides* – 2 species)

Figure 7. Pygmy woodlice (Family Trichoniscidae), all scale bars 1 mm

7a   Animal can roll into a tight ball (Fig. 7a), the only 'pygmy' wood-
(6a)   louse able to do this; maximum body length 3 mm; dorsal surface
        with large rounded longitudinal ridges; eyes each of three black
        ocelli (Fig. 8); body white; very rare . . . .
                                 Buddelundiella cataractae (p. 632)

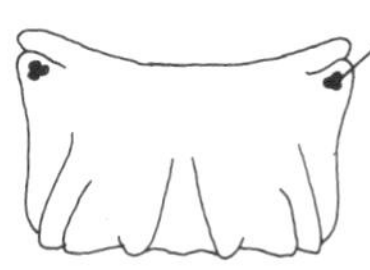

Figure 8.
Head (top view)

7b   Animal not able to roll into a ball; body up to 4 mm in length;
        dorsal surface with shallow longitudinal ridges; eyes each of one
        black ocellus (Fig. 7b); body white or pale creamy yellow
        (PLATE 2A, 2B); quite common. . . . .
                        Haplophthalmus (three species) . . . 8

8(7b) The genus *Haplophthalmus* contains three British species, one of which (*H. montivagus*) was discovered as recently as 1987. All three species are small, white, soil-dwelling woodlice which are very similar in appearance. They may be quite common in soil or under bark of damp rotting wood. Males and females of *H. danicus* can be separated from the other two species with a hand lens; the presence or absence of projections on the third *pleon* segment is a clear and reliable character. However, *H. mengei* and *H. montivagus* can be separated only after reference to the pleopods, and the arrangement of spines on the 7th legs of males. At present, there is no known way to distinguish between females of the latter two species. Figure 9 shows the rear half of the animals viewed from the right side, with the left legs omitted for clarity.

8a   Projections close to mid-line on dorsal surface of third segment of *pleon* are very
        feeble or absent (Fig. 9a); male first pleopod as in Fig. 10a . . . .
                                Haplophthalmus danicus (p. 634)

8b   Projections close to mid-line on dorsal surface of third segment of *pleon* are promi-
        nent (PLATE 2; Figs. 9b, 9c) 9

9   This couplet refers to mature males since females of the two species cannot (as yet) be
(8b)   separated. It is not possible to identify these two species when alive—they must
        be preserved in 70% alcohol. It is just possible, with a powerful hand lens, to see
        the pleopods in animals on their sides. However, a dissecting microscope is needed
        to see the spines on the legs. The difficulty of separating the two species has led to
        confusion in the past. Indeed, several of the records in Harding and Sutton (1985) for
        Haplophthalmus mengei from inland sites in southern England are, in fact, of *H. montivagus*.

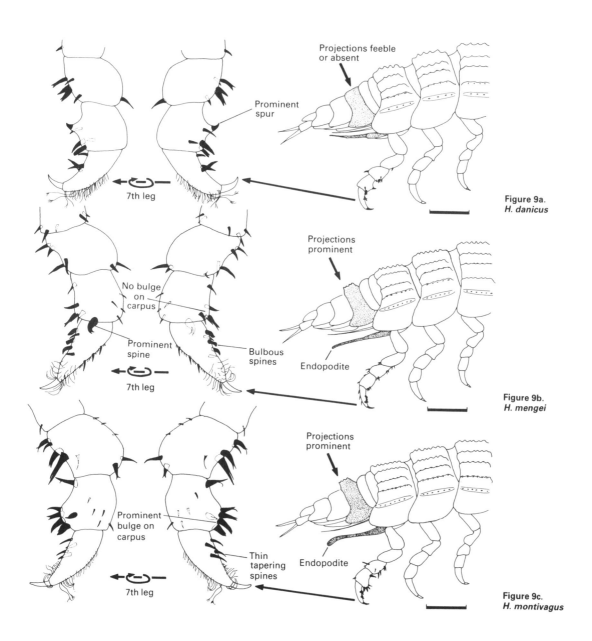

Figure 9. *Haplophthalmus* species (all scale bars 4 mm)

9a   Endopodites of first pleopods straight with narrow tips in animals seen from the side
      (Fig. 9b); arrangement of spines on 7th legs as in Fig. 9b with prominent spine on the
      inner face of the carpus; male first pleopod as in Fig. 10b . . . .
                                           Haplophthalmus mengei (p. 634)
                                                          (PLATE 2b)

9b   Endopodites of first pleopods curved strongly with expanded tips in animals seen
      from the side (like a round-ended banana—Fig. 9c); arrangement of spines on 7th
      legs as in Fig. 9c with prominent bulge on carpus; male first pleopod as in Fig. 10c .
                                         Haplophthalmus montivagus (p. 635)
                                                          (PLATE 2A)

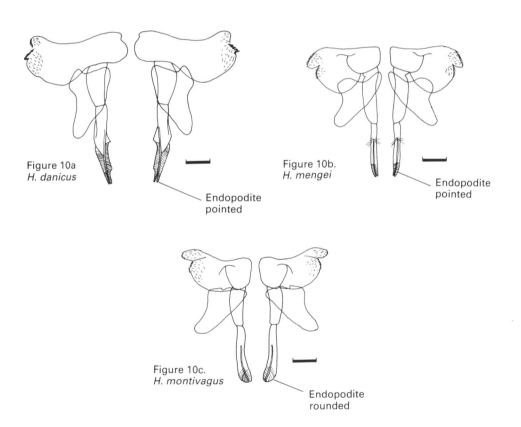

Figure 10. *Haplophthalmus* species.
Male first pleopods (all scale bars 0.1 mm)

10a   Dorsal surface smooth (Fig. 7c, 7e; PLATES 3A, 4A) 11
(6b)

10b   Dorsal surface with transverse rows of small bumps or spines (Fig. 7d, 7f, 7g;
      PLATES 2B, 3B, 5A) 13

11a   Eyes each of a single large brown ocellus (Fig. 7c); live animals
(10a) purple-maroon (PLATE 3A) and very fast moving; all body and
      eye pigments fade rapidly in 70% alcohol leaving animals a
      creamy yellow colour; up to 9 mm in length; SE Ireland only   .
                              Oritoniscus flavus (p. 638)
                                      (PLATE 3A)

3 ocelli

11b   Eyes of three black ocelli which do not fade in 70% alcohol (Fig.
      11); includes two species (Fig. 7e) which are widespread and
      common in the British Isles . . . .
                              Trichoniscus (two species) . . . 12

Figure 11.
Trichoniscus sp.
(Head from above)

12a   Body white or creamy white; maximum length 2.5 mm . . . .
(11b)   *Trichoniscus pygmaeus* (p. 645)

12b   Body coloured with reddish or purplish-brown pigments (occasionally bright
      purple—PLATE 4B) which do not fade in 70% alcohol; up to 5 mm in length   . .
                              Trichoniscus pusillus* (p. 645)
                                      (PLATE 4A, 4B)
                              Common pygmy woodlouse
                  *one of the 'famous five' very common species

NOTE: Separating juveniles of these species causes more problems in identification in the Isopod Survey
Scheme than all the others put together. However, juvenile *Trichoniscus pusillus* always contain some
reddish-brown pigment except when very young. Thus, creamy-white specimens of less than 2.5 mm in
length, with three ocelli forming a tight group on each side of the head, are invariably *T. pygmaeus*.

13a   Eyes of one black ocellus which does not fade in 70% alcohol (Figs. 7d, 7f, 12a, 12b)
(10b) 14

13b   Blind, or eyes of a single ocellus containing a red, orange or brown pigment which
      fades (often disappears completely) in 70% alcohol (Figs. 7g, 14a, 14b, 14c) . . 15

14a Eyes tiny in comparison to head size (Fig. 12a); antennae short (compare Fig. 12a
(13a) with 13); live animals completely white; maximum length 4 mm; male pleopods as in
      Fig. 12b,c; coastal sites only; quite rare . . . ***Miktoniscus patiencei*** (p. 637)

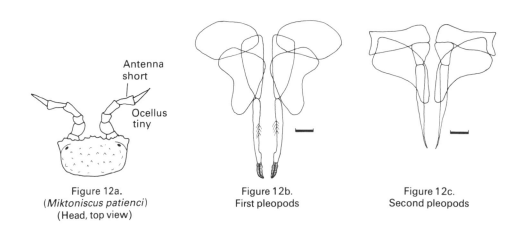

Figure 12a.
(*Miktoniscus patienci*)
(Head, top view)

Figure 12b.
First pleopods

Figure 12c.
Second pleopods

14b Eyes large in comparison to head size; antennae long (Fig. 13); live specimens usually
      a beautiful pink or rose red colour (PLATE 3B) (occasionally white) with a double
      yellow longitudinal stripe; in 70% alcohol, pink pigments disappear but
      eyes and yellow stripes remain prominent; maximum length 6 mm; widespread and
      common inland and on the coast . . . . . ***Androniscus dentiger*** (p. 630)
                                                              (PLATE 3B)
                                                          Rosy woodlouse

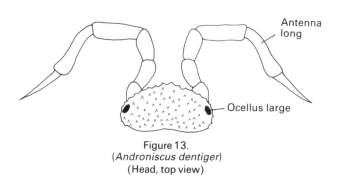

Figure 13.
(*Androniscus dentiger*)
(Head, top view)

NOTES

(key continues overleaf)

15   This group of woodlice contains six species. Their general
(13b) appearance is as Fig. 7g, although individuals may be longer and
more parallel-sided than the specimen shown in this drawing. All
are rarely encountered by beginners because of their small size (4
mm or less in length), and scarcity in the wild (although they are
certainly under-recorded). When alive, some species can be
identified provisionally from body and ocelli colour (if eyes are
present). However, after immersion in 70% alcohol the pigments
fade completely. Thus, the only certain means of identifying
preserved specimens is to examine the male pleopods. Preserved
females cannot (as yet) be identified.

Figure 14a.

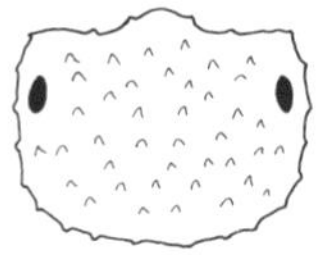

15a   Live specimens completely white (PLATE 2B) and blind (no
ocelli) (Fig. 14a); male first and second pleopods as Figs. 15a, 15b
Metatrichoniscoides (two species) 16

Figure 14b.

15b   Live specimens reddish-brown (PLATE 5A), or white tinted
with pale pink or orange, and eyes each of a single large reddish-
brown ocellus (Fig. 14b) or a small orange or red ocellus which
may be just a diffuse patch of pigment (Fig. 14c); all pigments
disappear in 70% alcohol; male first and second pleopods as Figs.
15c, d, e, f . . *Trichoniscoides* (four species) . . . 17

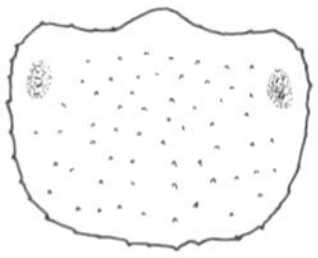

Figure 14c.

Figure 14. Heads
(top view)

16a   Male first and second pleopods as in Fig.15a . . . .
(15a)   *Metatrichoniscoides celticus* (p. 636)

16b   Male first and second pleopods as in Fig. 15b . . . .
                                 Metatrichoniscoides leydigi (p. 637)
                                                          (PLATE 2B)

Note: Platyarthrus hoffmannseggi (ant woodlouse) is the only other blind British woodlouse and may key
out here if the two distinct segments of the flagella of its antenna are mistaken for a single distinct segment
at couplet 3. However, *P. hoffmannseggi* is easily distinguished from the two *Metatrichoniscoides* species
since it is much broader in the body (cf. PLATE 2B and PLATE 5B).

17   Of the four species of *Trichoniscoides* now known to occur in Britain, *T. albidus*
(PLATE 5A) is the most widespread. *T. saeroeensis* is restricted to the coast and has
been recorded from more than 70 sites around the British Isles. *T. sarsi* has been
subject to mis-identification in the past and is known definitely only from gardens in
Dublin and Leicester, and churchyards in Kent—all synanthropic sites. Specimens
of *T. 'sarsi'* collected from woodlands have turned out to be *T. helveticus*, a species
which is widespread in north-west Europe. *Trichoniscoides helveticus* is known definitely from two woodlands near Oxford, a wood in Bedfordshire, and Didling Hill
in Sussex. On present knowledge, *T. sarsi* has all the signs of being a naturalised
introduction whereas *T. helveticus* is probably native to Britain.

17a   Body of live specimens reddish-brown (PLATE 5A) and eyes each of a single large
(15b) reddish-brown ocellus (Fig. 14b); all pigments fade to creamy-white in 70% alcohol;
male first and second pleopods as Fig. 15c .   *Trichoniscoides albidus* (p. 643)
                                                          (PLATE 5A)

17b   Body of live specimens white tinted with pale pink or orange and eyes each of a single
small orange or red ocellus (Fig. 14c); all pigments fade to white in 70% alcohol; male
first and second pleopods as Figs. 15d, e, f 18

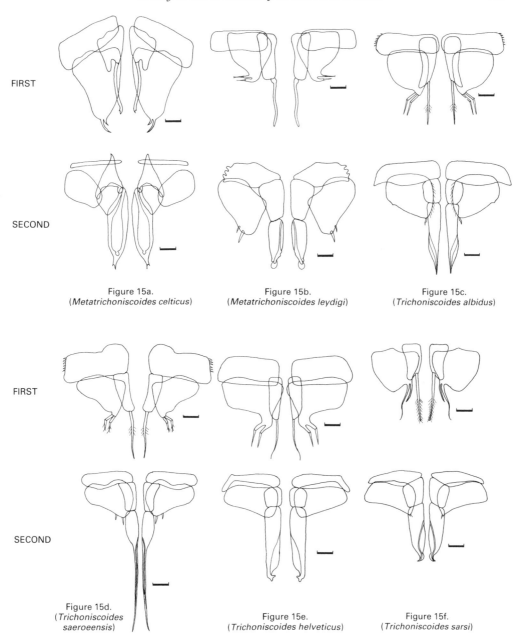

FIRST

SECOND

Figure 15a.
(*Metatrichoniscoides celticus*)

Figure 15b.
(*Metatrichoniscoides leydigi*)

Figure 15c.
(*Trichoniscoides albidus*)

FIRST

SECOND

Figure 15d.
(*Trichoniscoides
saeroeensis*)

Figure 15e.
(*Trichoniscoides helveticus*)

Figure 15f.
(*Trichoniscoides sarsi*)

Figure 15. Male pleopods (scale bars: Figures 15a–15b, 0.05 mm; Figures15c–15f, 0.1 mm)

18a   Endopodites of male second pleopods relatively long and narrow, tapering to fine
(17b) points (Fig. 15d); coastal sites only. . . ***Trichoniscoides saeroeensis*** (p. 644)

18b   Endopodites of male second pleopods relatively short and broad (Fig. 15e, f); not
        restricted to the coast 19

19a   Tips of endopodites of male second pleopods sickle-shaped (Fig. 15f) . . . . .
(18b)   ***Trichoniscoides sarsi*** (p. 644)

19b   Tips of endopodites of male second pleopods blunt, shaped like the end of an
        (African) elephant's trunk (Fig. 15e) . . ***Trichoniscoides helveticus*** (p. 643)

20a   Outline of edges of *pereon* and *pleon* a smooth line (Fig. 16a, inset); prominent lobes
(4a)   on either side of the head (Fig. 16a; PLATE 7A) . . ***Oniscus asellus*★** (p. 637)
                                                              (PLATES 6A, 7A)
                                                       Common shiny woodlouse
                                           ★One of the 'famous five' very common species

20b   Outline of edges of *pereon* and *pleon* a stepped line (Fig. 16b, c, d insets); no lobes on
        either side of the head 21

21a   Ground colour of body brown, greenish or pale yellow or red mottled with darker
(20b) pigmentation (PLATE 6A, 6B) which forms an obvious dark central stripe (Fig.
        16b); telson pointed (Fig. 16b); widespread and common in most habitats . . . .
                                                   ***Philoscia muscorum*★** (p. 638)
                                                              (PLATE 6B)
                                                   Common striped woodlouse
                                           ★One of the 'famous five' very common species

21b   Colour sandy brown without dark sandy stripe; telson rounded (Figs. 16c, d);
        seashore only; rare species 22

22a   Expopodites of uropods very long (Fig. 16c); total length of antennae from base to tip
(21b) about two thirds of the body length (PLATE 7B) . ***Halophiloscia couchi*** (p. 634)

22b   Expopodites of uropods short (Fig. 16d); total length of antennae from base to tip only
        about half of the body length (Fig. 16d) . . . ***Stenophiloscia zosterae*** (p. 642)

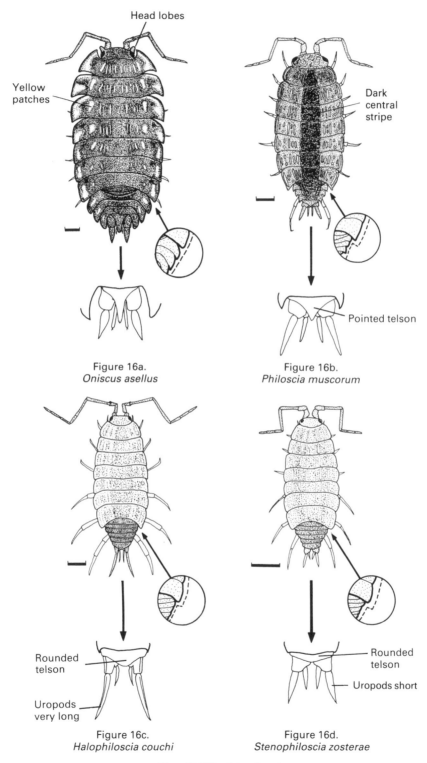

Figure 16a.
Oniscus asellus

Figure 16b.
Philoscia muscorum

Figure 16c.
Halophiloscia couchi

Figure 16d.
Stenophiloscia zosterae

Figure 16. (All scale bars 1 mm)

23a   Blind (no ocelli) (Fig. 17); completely white; maxi-
(4b)   mum length 4 mm; always associated with ants and
       often common in their nests .   .   .   .
                    Platyarthrus hoffmannseggi (p. 639)
                                              (PLATE 5B)
                                              Ant woodlouse

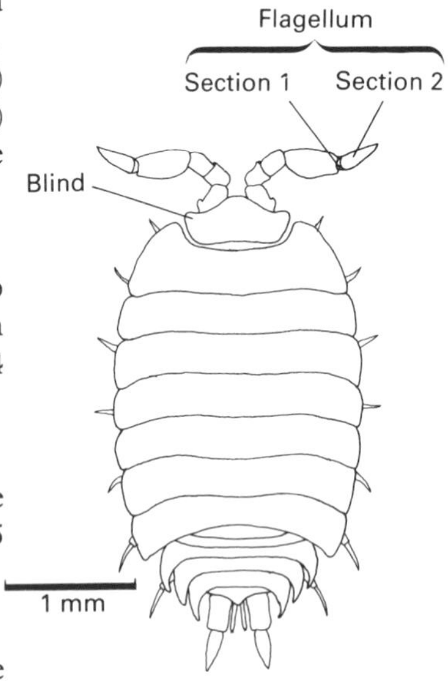

23b   Eyes each of several ocelli; body pigmented; up
       to 15 mm in length; not always associated with
       ants 24

24a   Outline of edges of *pereon* and *pleon* a smooth line
(23b)(Fig. 18a) 25

24b   Outline of edges of *pereon* and *pleon* a stepped line
       (Fig. 18b, c) .   .   .   .
                    Porcellionides (two species) .   .   . 30

Flagellum

Section 1   Section 2

Blind

1 mm

Figure 17. *Platyarthrus hoffmannseggi*

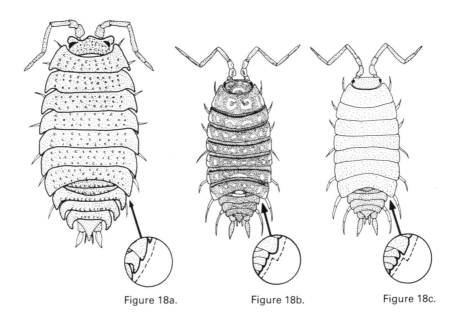

Figure 18a.   Figure 18b.   Figure 18c.

Figure 18.

25a Outline of body in cross section strongly arched (Fig. 19b); live specimens able to roll
(24a) into a ball with antennae folded over the dorsal surface (Fig. 19a, PLATE 8A)   . .
$$\textbf{\textit{Cylisticus convexus}} \text{ (p. 633)}$$
$$\text{(PLATE 8A)}$$

25b Outline of body in cross section not strongly arched (Fig. 19c); live specimens not
able to roll into a ball   26

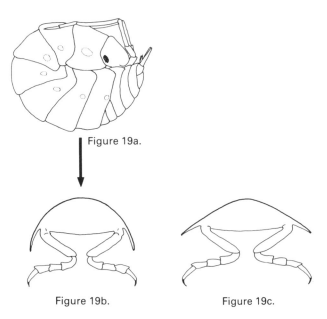

Figure 19a.

Figure 19b.   Figure 19c.

Figure 19.

26a Dorsal surface very smooth with no raised bumps; uropods long and tapering, widest
(25b) towards the end closest to the body (Fig. 20a, arrow); live animals appear distinctly
smooth and glossy (PLATE 9A); rare species   .   .   .   . ***Porcellio laevis*** (p. 640)
(PLATE 9A)

26b Dorsal surface covered in small raised bumps; uropods spear-shaped, widest about
half way along (Figs. 20b, c, arrows; Fig. 21a, b); live animals dull or slightly shiny
(never distinctly glossy)   27

27a Telson rounded at the tip (Fig. 20b; PLATE 10B)   . ***Porcellio dilatatus*** (p. 639)
(26b)   (PLATE 10A)

27b Telson pointed at the tip (Fig. 20c; Fig. 21)   28

NOTE: Adults of *Porcellio dilatatus* are much wider in comparison to their length than the other three
Porcellio species (compare Fig. 20b with Fig. 20a, c and 21a, and PLATE 10A with PLATE 9A and 11A).

28a   Head uniformly black and darker than the rest of the body (PLATE 9B) which has a
(27b) broken but distinct stripe down the middle (Fig. 20c); in live specimens, the stripe is
      almost always bordered with prominent yellow blotches which fade in 70% alcohol
                                                  Porcellio spinicornis (p. 640)

28b   Head colour similar to body which does not have a central dark stripe (Fig. 21a, b);
      live animals occasionally blotched with dull yellow patches but these are never
      arranged in rows either side of a dark central dark stripe and tend to occur all over the
      body   29

NOTE: *Porcellio spinicornis* bears a superficial resemblance to *Oniscus asellus* (PLATE 6A) in the field but
can be separated immediately by examining the pleopods. *P. spinicornis* has two pairs of lungs whereas
O. asellus has none.

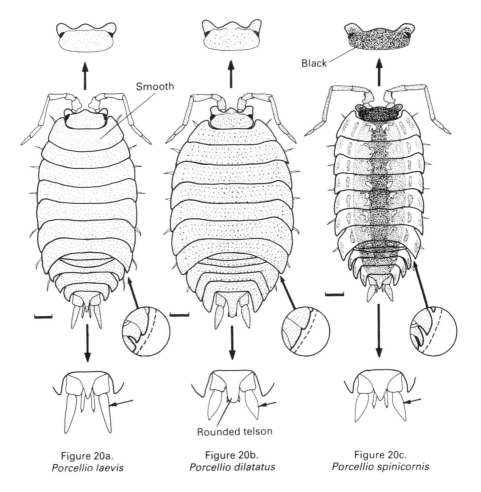

Figure 20a.
Porcellio laevis

Figure 20b.
Porcellio dilatatus

Figure 20c.
Porcellio spinicornis

Figure 20. (All scale bars 1 mm)
(the widest point of the uropods is indicated by an arrow)

29a   Posterior margin of first segment of the *pereon* more or less straight (Fig. 21a); two
(28b) pairs of lungs visible in live animals (not visible in 70% alcohol); very common
throughout Britain and Ireland . . . . **Porcellio scaber★** (p. 640)
(PLATE 11A)
Common rough woodlouse
★One of the 'Famous Five' very common species

29b   Posterior margin of first segment of *pereon* strongly curved (Fig. 21b); five pairs of
lungs visible in live animals (not visible in 70% alcohol); restricted to south-east
England and the Midlands . . . . **Trachelipus rathkei** (p. 642)
(PLATE 11B)

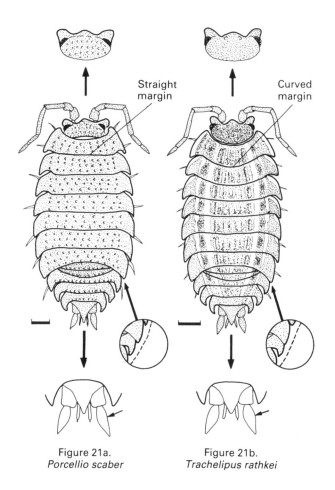

Straight margin

Curved margin

Figure 21a.
Porcellio scaber

Figure 21b.
Trachelipus rathkei

Figure 21. (Scale bars, 1 mm)
(the widest point of the uropods is indicated by an arrow)

30a Colour creamy-yellow to reddish-
(24b) brown mottled with brown and dark
grey (PLATE 12A); ridge running
across each segment of the *pereon*
(Fig. 22a). . . . .
Porcellionides cingendus (p. 641)
(PLATE 12A)

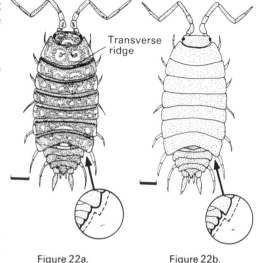

Transverse ridge

30b Colour uniform bluish-grey or occasionally orange; no ridges on the
pereon (Fig. 22b); live animals usually
covered in a bluish-grey 'bloom'
(PLATE 12B) which is easily rubbed
off, and which disappears in alcohol .
Porcellionides pruinosus (p. 641)
(PLATE 12B)

Figure 22a.
*Porcellionides
cingendus*

Figure 22b.
*Porcellionides
pruinosus*

Figure 22. (scale bars 1 mm)

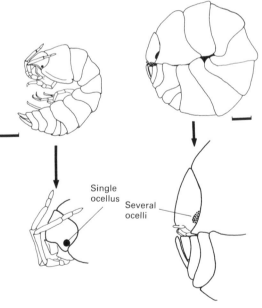

31a Eyes each composed of one prominent
(1b) ocellus (Fig. 23a) . . . .
Eluma purpurascens (p. 633)
(PLATE 13A)

Single
ocellus

Several
ocelli

31b Eyes each composed of several ocelli
(Fig. 23b) . . . **Armadillidium**
(six species, Fig. 25) . . . 32

Figure 23a.
Eluma purpurascens

Figure 23b.
Armadillidium vulgare

Figure 23. Heads (seen from left side) (scale bars 1 mm)

32a   Live animals are pale sandy colour (PLATE 13B) which fades to white in 70%
(31b) alcohol; maximum length 6 mm; dorsal surface covered in tiny spines (Fig. 25f, most
      obvious in dry specimens); male 7th legs with knob on basis (Fig. 25x); rare; sea shore
      only, restricted to the strand line of sandy beaches and salt marshes . . . . . .
      Armadillidium album (p. 630)
      (PLATE 13B)

32b   Live animals are uniform slate grey, pink or brown, or mottled with yellow, black,
      brown or orange pigments which fade slightly in 70% alcohol; some species up to
      20 mm in length; dorsal surface smooth (Fig. 25a–e); male 7th legs without knob on
      basis (Fig. 25s–w); not restricted to the sea shore 33

33a   Scutellum on forehead formed into a very distinct 'snout-like' process which projects
(32b) well above the head between antennae (Fig. 25i); live animals leave antennae folded
      over the dorsal surface when they roll into a ball (Fig. 25c) . . . .
      Armadillidium nasatum (p. 631)

Note: orientate the animal so that you are looking at it 'face-on'; good lighting will help here.

33b   Scutellum on forehead not formed into an obvious 'snout-like' projection (Figs. 25g,
      h, j, k); live animals fold antennae inside the 'ball' when they roll up (Figs. 25a, b, d)
      34

34a   Posterior edge of first pereonite chamfered (cut-off) (Fig. 25d, arrow; PLATE 14A);
(33b) maximum length 5 mm; tip of telson wide in comparison to height (Fig. 25p); male
      7th legs with fringe of 'hairs' on the anterior face of the ischium (Fig. 25v); ridge on
      scutellum extends all the way around 'face' (Fig. 25j). . . . .
      Armadillidium pulchellum (p. 632)
      (PLATE 14A)

Note: In preserved specimens of *Armadillidium pulchellum* and *A. pictum*, a strongly pigmented patch
remains on the edge of the 7th pereonite when other pigmentation fades slightly (Fig. 25d, e).

34b   Posterior edge of first pereonite not chamfered (Figs. 25a, b, e); some species up to
      20 mm in length; tip of telson narrow in comparison to height (Fig. 25m, n, q); 7th
      legs without fringe of 'hairs' on the anterior face of the ischium (Fig. 25s, t, w); ridge
      on scutellum does not extend all the way around 'face' (Fig. 25g, h, k) 35

35a   Live animals leave a gap when rolled up due to their inability to form a perfect sphere
(34b)(Fig. 25b; PLATE 15B) and often rest in a clamped position (PLATE 15A) in which
they remain, even when disturbed; scutellum projects slightly above the top of the
head (Fig. 25h); pleonites appear 'splayed out' like a skirt when viewed from behind
(Fig. 25n) . . . .   ***Armadillidium depressum*** (p. 630)
(PLATE 15A, B)

35b   Live animals form a perfect sphere when rolled up, with no gap (Fig. 25a, e;
PLATES 14B, 16A, 16B) and almost always roll into a ball when disturbed;
scutellum does not project above the top of the head (Fig. 25g, k); pleonites appear
'tucked in' when viewed from behind (Fig. 25m, q) 36

36a   Live animals dark brown or black with attractive yellow or greenish mottling
(PLATE 14B); specimens preserved in 70% alcohol are mottled dark grey with a
solid patch of pigment on the edges of the 7th pereonite (Fig. 25e) (this is also present
in *A. pulchellum*, Fig. 25d); maximum length 9 mm; male pleopods as Fig. 24b;
extremely rare species . . . .   ***Armadillidium pictum*** (p. 631)
(PLATE 14B)

36b   Colour of live and preserved specimens usually uniform slate grey, brown, pink or
black but if mottled, then without a dark solid patch of pigment on the edges of
the 7th pereonite (Fig. 25a); up to 18 mm in length; male pleopods as Fig. 24a;
extremely common in south and east England and Ireland but much more coastal and
synanthropic north and west of these areas .   ***Armadillidium vulgare*** *(p. 632)
(PLATE 16A, 16B)
*One of the 'famous five' very common species

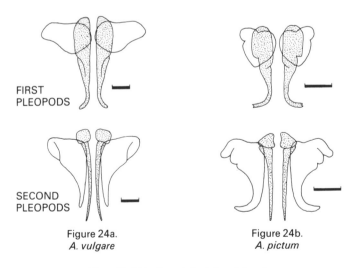

FIRST
PLEOPODS

SECOND
PLEOPODS

Figure 24a.
A. vulgare

Figure 24b.
A. pictum

Figure 24. Male pleopods (scale bars 0.5 mm)

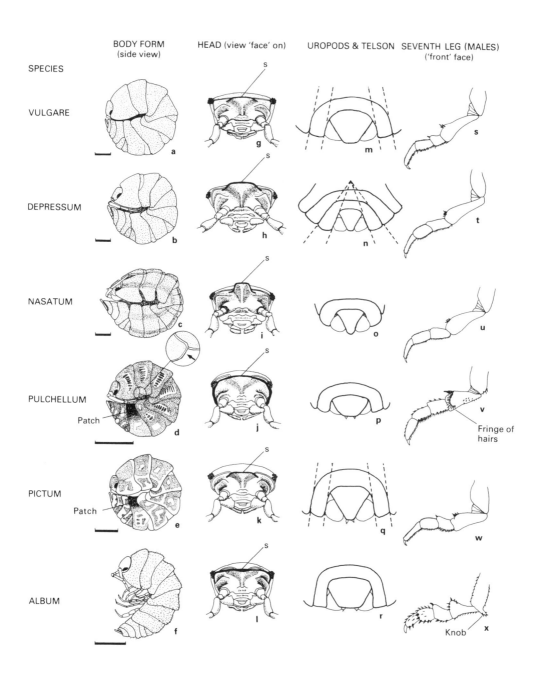

Figure 25. *Armadillidium* spp. (scale bars 1 mm) (s = scutellum viewed from in front)

Species Descriptions

Androniscus dentiger (Rosy woodlouse)
(PLATE 3B)

Maximum length:	6 mm
Colour in life:	Pink to rose red with double yellow stripe down the centre of the body (Fig. 7f). Occasionally, populations composed of white or very pale pink individuals occur (usually in caves or mines).
Eyes:	Each of a single large black ocellus (Fig. 12b).
Lungs:	None.
Behaviour:	Moves rapidly when disturbed.
Preserved:	Body pigments fade completely but black pigment in ocelli remains. The double yellow stripe is sometimes visible through the cuticle as a pair of long pale yellow bodies on either side of the gut.
Habitat:	Wide range of natural and synanthropic sites including scree slopes inland and on the coast, garden rubble, old quarries etc. Sometimes found in streams completely submerged.
Distribution:	Widespread and common throughout Britain and Ireland.
Comments:	This is a highly distinctive species which is unlikely to be confused with any other British woodlouse. In my opinion, the most attractive British species.

Armadillidium album
(PLATE 13B)

Maximum length:	6 mm
Colour in life:	Pale sand.
Eyes:	Each of numerous black ocelli
Lungs:	Two pairs.
Behaviour:	May roll into a ball when disturbed but usually leaves a gap. The posture in PLATE 13B is characteristic.
Preserved:	All body pigments fade (hence specific name *album* = white) but black ocelli remain prominent.
Habitat:	Drift line of sandy beaches and salt marshes, often found under driftwood.
Distribution:	Rare. Known from about a dozen sites around the coast of England and Wales, three sites on the east coast of Ireland and one site in south-west Scotland and the Isle of Man.
Comments:	Quite a difficult species to find as it is the same colour as sand. *A. album* is highly tolerant of immersion in seawater, reproduces in summer and lives for two years (Vader and De Wolf, 1988).

Armadillidium depressum
(PLATE 15A, 15B)

Maximum length:	20 mm
Colour in life:	Uniform slate grey, often with longitudinal rows of yellow blotches, especially in juveniles.
Eyes:	Each of numerous black ocelli.
Lungs:	Two pairs.
Behaviour:	More prone to 'clamping' to substratum than the other pill woodlice (PLATE 15A). Rolls into an imperfect sphere (PLATE 15B; Fig. 25b).

Preserved: Yellow blotches (if present) fade but grey colour remains.

Habitat: Coastal cliffs and a wide range of synanthropic sites inland. Very resistant to drying out—I have often encountered this species crawling over stones in full sunlight in mid summer.

Distribution: Locally abundant in south west England and South Wales.

Comments: *A. depressum* is especially common in gardens in Bristol, Bath, Cardiff and other towns and cities in this area where it often enters houses. Rare to the north and east of a line from Aberystwyth through Cheltenham to the Isle of Wight, but it should be looked for outside these areas. Some recent records suggest that it may be spreading its range. The species has not been found in Scotland and Ireland. *A. depressum* is more easily identified alive by the way it rolls up than dead. Sutton and Harding (1989) have suggested that it may be an old introduction to England.

Armadillidium nasatum
(Fig. 25c)

Maximum length: 20 mm

Colour in life: Greyish-brown with a 'translucent' appearance and longitudinal bands of darker mottling (Fig. 25c).

Eyes: Each of numerous black ocelli.

Lungs: Two pairs.

Behaviour: Rolls into a slightly flattened sphere when disturbed but leaves its antennae protruding over the dorsal surface (Fig. 25c—similar behaviour to *Cylisticus convexus*—PLATE 8A).

Preserved: Colour fades slightly.

Habitat: Likes sunny spots in old quarries, gardens, exposed grassland etc. It is sometimes abundant in glasshouses and I have found this species indoors and outdoors in most garden centres.

Distribution: Locally common in England and Wales south of a line between Aberystwyth and Hull. Absent from northern England and Scotland. The only recent record from Ireland is from the Dublin area.

Comments: The projection on the head (Fig. 25i) is very obvious and this species is unlikely to be confused with any other pill woodlouse.

Armadillidium pictum
(PLATE 14B)

Maximum length: 9 mm

Colour in life: Black, attractively mottled with yellow patches.

Eyes: Each of numerous black ocelli.

Lungs: Two pairs.

Behaviour: Rolls into a perfect sphere when disturbed (PLATE 14B; Fig. 25e).

Preserved: Colour fades to a mottled grey (darker than in *Armadillidium pulchellum*) with a solid patch of pigment remaining on the edges of the 7th pereonite (Fig. 25e). Male first and second pleopods as Fig. 24b.

Habitat: Ancient woodland, mountain screes, upland limestone areas.

Distribution: Almost certainly the rarest woodlouse in Britain. Apart from two sites in the Lake District, where single specimens have been found, it is only known to occur in numbers in two sites in mid-Wales in woodland and mountain scree, and two sites on limestone in north-west England (Richardson, 1989).

Comments: *A. pictum* is the only species of woodlouse to be considered as worthy of listing in the British non-insect red data book of threatened species.

Armadillidium pulchellum
(PLATE 14A)

Maximum length: 5 mm
Colour in life: Dark brown, attractively mottled with yellow, chestnut and orange patches.
Eyes: Each of numerous black ocelli.
Lungs: Two pairs.
Behaviour: Rolls into a ball when disturbed but leaves a slight gap (Fig. 25d).
Preserved: Colour fades to mottled grey (lighter than *Armadillidium pictum*) with a solid patch of pigment remaining on the edges of the 7th pereonite (Fig. 25d).
Habitat: Difficult to generalise but most records are from natural sites in grassland under limestone rocks etc. The species seems to be very resistant to drying out and is sometimes found in ants' nests.
Distribution: A species with a 'north-west bias' to its distribution. Currently known from about 80 sites in Wales, Ireland, northern England and southern Scotland but recent records from north Cornwall and Devon and a conifer plantation in north Hampshire suggest that it is probably much more widespread. A characteristic species of coastal cliffs in west Wales.
Comments: *A. pulchellum* was originally thought to be very rare but records in recent years have increased substantially as the number of collectors able to recognise this inconspicuous and attractive species in the field has increased. Quite an easy species to keep in culture. I have maintained a population in the laboratory for six years.

Armadillidium vulgare (Common pill woodlouse)
(PLATE 16A, 16B)

Maximum length: 18 mm
Colour in life: Uniform slate grey, pink, red or brown. Mottled specimens are sometimes found, most often near the sea.
Eyes: Each of numerous black ocelli.
Lungs: Two pairs.
Behaviour: Rolls into a perfect sphere when disturbed (PLATE 16A; Fig. 25a).
Preserved: Colour fades slightly. Male first and second pleopods as Fig. 24a.
Habitat: Wide range of natural and synanthropic sites.
Distribution: Extremely common in south and east England and Ireland but is much more coastal and synanthropic north and west of these areas. Absent from central Northern England.
Comments: *A. vulgare* can be easily separated from the other two common species of pill woodlouse in the field by the way in which it rolls into a completely enclosed sphere (Fig. 25a). *A. depressum* (Fig. 25b) and *A. nasatum* (Fig. 25c) both leave a gap, the latter with its antennae held over the dorsal surface.

Buddelundiella cataractae
(Fig. 7a)

Maximum length: 3 mm
Colour in life: White or buff.

Eyes:	Each of three black ocelli (Fig. 8).
Lungs:	None.
Behaviour:	Rolls into a tight ball and resembles a sand grain to the naked eye.
Preserved:	Fades to white but black ocelli remain prominent.
Habitat:	Coastal shingle banks and under stones in gardens.
Distribution:	Discovered in South Wales in 1981 (Oliver, 1983). So far, known only from coastal sites in north Norfolk and South Wales, a garden in Cardiff and a garden centre near Oxford.
Comments:	This species is very inconspicuous in the field and may prove to be more common than current records would indicate. The best technique for collecting this species is to spread humus out on a tray and examine under a strong light. A more comprehensive description of this species is given in Harding and Sutton (1985).

Cylisticus convexus
(PLATE 8A, 8B)

Maximum length:	15 mm
Colour in life:	Pale greyish-brown, often with much paler grey or orange uropods.
Eyes:	Each of numerous dark grey ocelli.
Lungs:	Five pairs (PLATE 8B). Only one other species, *Trachelipus rathkei* (PLATE 11B) has five pairs of lungs.
Behaviour:	Runs very fast when disturbed. If picked up, this species will roll into an imperfect slightly flattened sphere with its prominent uropods and antennae projecting (PLATE 8A).
Preserved:	Body colour fades slightly and uropods and telson become white.
Habitat:	May be abundant on the coast among debris at the base of eroding cliffs and other sites subject to disturbance. Inland, found almost exclusively in synanthropic sites (rubbish tips, old quarries, etc.).
Distribution:	Locally common throughout Britain and Ireland.
Comments:	*C. convexus* may initially be confused with *Armadillidium nasatum* which also leaves its antennae projecting over the dorsal surface when it rolls up (Fig. 25c). However, the prominent pointed uropods and telson of *C. convexus* (Fig. 19a) easily separate this species from the 'true' pill woodlice with their spade-like uropods and telson (Fig. 25m–r).

Eluma purpurascens
(PLATE 13A)

Maximum length:	Usually 10 mm (rarely up to 15 mm)
Colour in life:	Purplish brown, clothed in a 'bloom' of tiny 'hairs' (PLATE 13A).
Eyes:	Each of one large black ocellus (Fig. 23a).
Lungs:	Two pairs.
Behaviour:	Rolls into a ball when disturbed but usually leaves a gap. The posture shown in PLATE 13A is characteristic.
Preserved:	Becomes greyish. Hairs very difficult to see.
Habitat:	Coastal cliffs and inland synanthropic sites.
Distribution:	In Ireland, common along the coast near Dublin and at two inland sites. In England, Harding and Sutton (1985) reported the species from two sites, one in east Norfolk and the other near Herne Bay, east Kent. However, in the last few years, it has been found in about a dozen further locations in Kent.

Comments: *E. purpurascens* has apparently become more common in recent years and may
                   be an introduction which is spreading its range.

Halophiloscia couchi
(PLATE 7B)

Maximum length: 10 mm
Colour in life: Pale pinkish-brown.
Eyes: Each of numerous black ocelli.
Lungs: None.
Behaviour: Runs very fast when disturbed.
Preserved: Colour fades to pale greyish-brown.
Habitat: Hides during daylight in crevices in shingle and boulder beaches, and among
                   debris at the base of eroding cliffs. Also found on the shores of tidal rivers. It
                   emerges at night to feed.
Distribution: Southern and western coasts of England and Wales with St. Bees and Dover as
                   the northern and eastern extremes respectively. In Ireland, known only from
                   Howth near Dublin.
Comments: This species may be confused with juvenile specimens of the common sea
                   slater *Ligia oceanica* in the field. However, the antennae (PLATE 7B) are
                   highly characteristic and prevent confusion with any other British woodlouse.

Haplophthalmus danicus
(Fig. 7b)

Maximum length: 4 mm
Colour in life: White or pale cream-yellow with dull surface.
Eyes: Each of one black ocellus.
Lungs: None.
Behaviour: Walks slowly when disturbed. Never has the rapid darting motion of running
                   woodlice.
Preserved: Black ocelli remain prominent. Male first pleopods as Fig. 10a.
Habitat: Rotting wood, humus, rubbish tips, and a wide range of damp sites.
Distribution: Probably widespread in Ireland, Wales and England south of a line between
                   the Mersey and the Humber.
Comments: Under recorded. Numerous recent records for this species indicate that it is
                   more common than suggested by Harding and Sutton (1985). The absence of
                   projections on the dorsal surface of the third pleonite (Fig. 9a) is a reliable
                   character for separating this species from *H. mengei* and *H. montivagus*
                   (Figs. 9b, 9c).

Haplophthalmus mengei
(PLATE 2B, Fig. 7b)

Maximum length: 4 mm
Colour in life: White or pale cream-yellow with dull surface.
Eyes: Each of one black ocellus.
Lungs: None.
Behaviour: Walks slowly when disturbed. Never has the rapid darting motion of running
                   woodlice.

Preserved: Black ocelli remain prominent.

Habitat: Similar sites to *H. danicus* with which it is often found. Perhaps more common than *H. danicus* near the coast.

Distribution: Widespread in Ireland, but under recorded in England. Probably widespread in England and Wales. Its range overlaps with that of *H. montivagus* in central southern England but to date, both species have not been found together in the same microhabitat. The closest they get is at Little Wittenham Wood near Dorchester where *H. mengei* occurs only in riverside meadows and *H. montivagus* is restricted to the woodland above the flood plain.

Comments: The difficulty of separating this species from *H. montivagus* has led to confusion in the past. Indeed several of the records in Harding and Sutton (1985) for *H. mengei* from inland sites in southern England are, in fact, of *H. montivagus*.

Haplophthalmus montivagus
(PLATE 2A, Fig. 7b)

Maximum length: 4 mm

Colour in life: White or pale cream-yellow with dull surface.

Eyes: Each of one black ocellus.

Lungs: None.

Behaviour: Walks slowly when disturbed. Never has the rapid darting motion of running woodlice.

Preserved: Black ocelli remain prominent.

Habitat: Under stones and in rotting wood showing a distinct preference for ancient woodlands on calcareous soils. Not yet found on the coast.

Distribution: Known from eight sites in central southern England including a wooded limestone quarry near Bath, a woodland on chalk near Luton, and Wytham Wood near Oxford. At Little Wittenham Wood near Dorchester, it occurs quite close to *H. mengei* but not in the same microhabitat (see notes on Distribution under *H. mengei* above).

Comments: This species was discovered in 1987 by examining reference collections of *H. 'mengei'* in which *H. montivagus* had been hiding for at least 20 years. *H. montivagus* is quite well known in Europe (Gruner, 1966). Numerous other species of *Haplophthalmus* have been described (Vandel, 1960). However, several of these 'species' have been separated on the basis of very subtle differences in the orientation of spines on the 7th legs of males, and on the shape of the tip of the endopodite of the male first pleopods. These characters show variation between individuals of the same species. Thus, the number of true species of *Haplophthalmus* in Europe is probably considerably less than that described by Vandel (1960, 1962). Hopkin and Roberts (1987) provides a more detailed discussion of the validity of Vandel's 'species'.

Ligia oceanica (Common sea slater)
(PLATE 1A,1B)

Maximum length: 30 mm

Colour in life: Greenish-grey to uniform light grey-brown. The colour can be altered to suit that of the background by expansion or contraction of specialised cells under the cuticle (melanocytes) which contain a black pigment (melanin) (Willmer *et al.*, 1989).

Eyes:	Large, each of numerous ocelli (PLATE 1B), similar in appearance to the 'compound' eye of insects.
Lungs:	None.
Behaviour:	Runs extremely rapidly when disturbed.
Preserved:	Body colour fades to a uniform cream colour but eyes remain prominent.
Habitat:	Sea shore only. Hides in crevices on rocky shores during the day emerging at night to graze on seaweed and other algae. Occurs also on man-made substrates such as harbour walls, wooden piles and seawalls on 'soft' coasts and has even occurred in strandlines on sand beaches.
Distribution:	Very common on rocky shores around the entire coast of Britain and Ireland.
Comments:	Easily the largest British woodlouse and quite an impressive animal when fully grown. *L. oceanica* is used extensively, in teaching, to study the basis of colour change in Crustacea. It is also cooked and eaten on survival courses. One member of the British Isopod Study Group who has consumed *Ligia* found them rather unappetising.

Ligidium hypnorum
(Fig. 6b)

Maximum length:	9 mm
Colour in life:	Dark mottled brown with shiny dorsal surface. Very occasionally purple if infected with the iridovirus (*cf.* PLATE 4B).
Eyes:	Large, each of numerous black ocelli (Fig. 5a), similar in appearance to the 'compound' eye of insects.
Lungs:	None.
Behaviour:	Runs extremely rapidly when disturbed.
Preserved:	Body colour fades slightly but black eyes remain prominent.
Habitat:	Damp leaf litter in fens and deciduous (often ancient) woods.
Distribution:	Locally common in south and east England.
Comments:	Possibly an ancient woodland 'indicator' species. Considering its 'primitive' features (antennal flagellum with many segments, eyes of 100 or more ocelli) *L. hypnorum* is surprisingly tolerant of dry conditions.

Metatrichoniscoides celticus
(Similar in appearance to *M. leydigi*—PLATE 2B)

Maximum length:	3 mm
Colour in life:	White.
Eyes:	Blind (Fig. 14a).
Lungs:	None.
Behaviour:	Moves slowly when disturbed.
Preserved:	White. The only certain way to distinguish preserved specimens of this species from *Metatrichoniscoides leydigi* and the four species of *Trichoniscoides* is by comparing male first and second pleopods (Figs. 15a–f).
Habitat:	Under stones, in strandline debris etc.
Distribution:	Discovered on the coast of South Wales in 1979 where it has been found in seven sites in strandline debris, or under deeply-embedded boulders on eroding turf. These were the only sites known to Harding and Sutton (1985) but since then, the species has been found inland under stones in a limestone quarry in South Wales, and single females, possibly of this species, have turned

up on the Giant's Causeway in Northern Ireland and at St. Bees in Cumbria. These recent records suggest that it is widespread and waiting to be discovered at many sites throughout Britain and Ireland.

Comments: *M. celticus* probably occurs elsewhere in Europe where it may be known under a different name. A more comprehensive description of this species is given in Harding and Sutton (1985), and Oliver and Trew (1981).

Metatrichoniscoides leydigi
(PLATE 2B)

Maximum length:	3 mm
Colour in life:	White.
Eyes:	Blind (Fig. 14a).
Lungs:	None.
Behaviour:	Moves slowly when disturbed.
Preserved:	White. The only certain way to distinguish preserved specimens of this species from *Metatrichoniscoides celticus* and the four species of *Trichoniscoides* is by comparing male first and second pleopods (Figs. 15a–f).
Habitat:	Under stones, plant pots etc.
Distribution:	Discovered in a garden centre near Oxford in 1989, well away from glasshouses.
Comments:	This species is almost certainly present in other similar places in Britain, but to date is still only known from the one site.

Miktoniscus patiencei
(Fig. 7d)

Maximum length:	4 mm
Colour in life:	White.
Eyes:	Each of a single tiny black ocellus (Fig. 12a).
Lungs:	None.
Behaviour:	Moves slowly when disturbed.
Preserved:	White. Gut contents often show through the cuticle. Male pleopods as Figs. 12b, c.
Habitat:	Plant litter in salt marshes or near high tide mark at the base of cliffs in soil-filled cracks or on stable shingle.
Distribution:	Scattered records, mainly from the south coast of England and Ireland. Recent records from north-east Scotland, East Anglia and North Wales suggest that it is probably widespread around the coast of Britain and Ireland.
Comments:	Discovered on the coast of Cornwall and the Isle of Wight in 1976. The tiny jet black ocellus on each side of the head is highly characteristic. A more comprehensive description of this species is given in Harding and Sutton (1985) and Oliver and Sutton (1982).

Oniscus asellus (Common shiny woodlouse)
(PLATES 6A, 7A)

Maximum length:	16 mm
Colour in life:	Usually shiny and grey with irregular light markings and two rows of yellow patches. Yellow and orange forms are known, especially near the sea. Juveniles

are usually less shiny than adults. Very occasionally purple if infected with the iridovirus (*cf*. PLATE 4B).

Eyes:	Each of numerous black ocelli.
Lungs:	None.
Behaviour:	Initially remains motionless when disturbed and may be difficult to dislodge due to its flattened shape and relatively smooth body surface. It runs quite fast when provoked to do so.
Preserved:	Colour fades slightly.
Habitat:	Found in almost every habitat where conditions are damp, particularly under rotting wood in deciduous woodlands. It occurs often with *Porcellio scaber* on compost heaps and in garden refuse.
Distribution:	Extremely common throughout Britain and Ireland.
Comments:	The colour and shape of *O. asellus* are quite variable but the presence of three segments in the antennal flagellum and the prominent head lobes (PLATE 7A) make it unlikely that this species will be confused with any other in Britain. Together with *Porcellio scaber* (the common rough woodlouse), this is one of the most widespread and abundant invertebrates in Britain.

Oritoniscus flavus
(PLATE 3A)

Maximum length:	9 mm
Colour in life:	Purple-maroon and very shiny.
Eyes:	Each of one large dark brown ocellus.
Lungs:	None.
Behaviour:	Possibly the fastest running of all woodlice and difficult to catch in the field.
Preserved:	Eye pigments fade but ocelli can still be seen easily. The body colour fades to cream-yellow (hence specific name *flavus* = yellow).
Habitat:	Under stones, in leaf litter, rubbish etc. and invariably less than 20 m from a river.
Distribution:	South-east Ireland only.
Comments:	*O. flavus* has not been found in mainland Britain despite extensive searches of potentially suitable sites by experienced recorders. It may have crossed into Ireland via a land bridge soon after the retreat of the ice sheet following the last glaciation, and then died out possibly through competition, in all but its present stronghold. Perhaps *O. flavus* is eaten by snakes!

Philoscia muscorum (Common striped woodlouse)
(PLATE 6B)

Maximum length:	11 mm
Colour in life:	Shiny mottled brown with a dark stripe down the centre of the body. Bright yellow, red and greenish forms are quite common. Very occasionally purple if infected with the iridovirus (*cf*. PLATE 4B).
Eyes:	Each of numerous black ocelli.
Lungs:	None.
Behaviour:	Runs fast when disturbed and feels 'soft to the touch' when picked up.
Preserved:	Colour fades slightly but central dark stripe remains.
Habitat:	Particularly common in hedgerows and grassland at the base of tussocks but can also be found in gardens and woodlands.
Distribution:	Common throughout Britain and Ireland.

Comments: Most populations of *P. muscorum* contain individuals of a range of colours (PLATE 6B). Near the sea, the yellow form tends to dominate. This species is less common in gardens than *Oniscus asellus* (common shiny woodlouse) and *Porcellio scaber* (common rough woodlouse) but in grassland, it is probably the dominant species of woodlouse in most areas. *P. muscorum* has been studied extensively by Sutton and co-workers in a long-running research project on dune grassland at Spurn Head in Yorkshire (see *e.g.* Sutton *et al.*, 1984, Grundy and Sutton, 1989).

Platyarthrus hoffmannseggi (Ant woodlouse)
(PLATE 5B)

Maximum length:	4 mm
Colour in life:	White. Gut contents often show through the cuticle.
Eyes:	Blind.
Lungs:	None.
Behaviour:	Runs amongst ants when disturbed and vibrates its antennae from side to side very rapidly.
Preserved:	Same colour as in life. The body is very broad in comparison to its length (Fig. 17).
Habitat:	Lives in close association with ants and is found frequently in their nests.
Distribution:	Common in nests of most species of ant in Wales and southern England (Hames, 1987), but becomes more scattered north of a line through Liverpool and Hull. There are no recent records from Scotland. In Ireland, confined to the south-east.
Comments:	In ant nests, *P. hoffmannseggi* probably feeds on pellets regurgitated by its hosts (Williams and Franks, 1988). In Malaysia, a similar species in the genus *Exalloniscus* can be found attached to the pupae of ponerine army ants from which they hitch a ride.

Porcellio dilatatus
(PLATE 10A)

Maximum length:	15 mm
Colour in life:	Dull greyish-brown with a 'translucent' sheen which is difficult to describe (and photograph!) but which experienced isopodologists can recognise in the field immediately. Pale broad longitudinal stripes are present either side of the midline which are more obvious in younger specimens.
Eyes:	Each of numerous black ocelli.
Lungs:	Two pairs.
Behaviour:	Initially remains motionless but runs away quite rapidly when disturbed.
Preserved:	Colour fades slightly.
Habitat:	Found in a range of natural and synanthropic sites where it can be locally abundant, particularly on farms with dairy herds and old brick buildings.
Distribution:	Scattered records from most parts of Britain and Ireland. This is quite a rare species but is probably under-recorded due to confusion with the much more common *Porcellio scaber*.
Comments:	The shape of the telson in adults of this species is highly distinctive (PLATE 10B). In younger specimens this character is not so obvious but the tip of the telson is still more rounded than in the other *Porcellio* species. *P. dilatatus* may be parthenogenetic and is very easy to keep in culture.

Porcellio laevis
(PLATE 9A)

Maximum length:	18 mm
Colour in life:	Glossy brownish-grey.
Eyes:	Each of numerous black ocelli.
Lungs:	Two pairs.
Behaviour:	Initially remains motionless but runs away quite rapidly when disturbed.
Preserved:	Colour fades slightly.
Habitat:	Found mostly in synanthropic sites (old compost heaps, gardens etc.) where if found, it is usually abundant such as on the compost heap of Oxford Botanic Gardens and eroding gardens on the cliffs at Swanage.
Distribution:	Rare. Known from only about 20 sites scattered across eastern and southern England and the Dublin area of Ireland. It has yet to be recorded from Wales or Scotland.
Comments:	The dorsal surface of this species is very smooth and is best felt by rubbing a fingertip from the back to the front of a specimen. The other *Porcellio* species feel 'rough' to the touch, particularly *Porcellio scaber* (the common rough woodlouse). The uropods are also distinctive being more tapering than the spear-shaped uropods of the other *Porcellio* species (Fig. 20a).

Porcellio scaber (Common rough woodlouse)
(PLATE 11A)

Maximum length:	17 mm
Colour in life:	Usually slate-grey, but orange and cream forms speckled with black, red or brown are often found, especially near the sea.
Eyes:	Each of numerous black ocelli.
Lungs:	Two pairs.
Behaviour:	Initially remains motionless but runs away quite rapidly when disturbed.
Preserved:	Any orange colour vanishes but other pigments fade only slightly.
Habitat:	Found in a wide range of habitats. It tends to prefer slightly drier conditions than the equally common *Oniscus asellus*, with which it is often found on compost heaps.
Distribution:	Very common throughout Britain and Ireland.
Comments:	*P. scaber* and the common shiny woodlouse *Oniscus asellus* are the most widespread and common species in Britain. *P. scaber* has a greater tendency to enter houses.

Porcellio spinicornis
(PLATE 9B, Fig. 20c)

Maximum length:	12 mm
Colour in life:	Black head with body marked attractively with a row of bright yellow blotches on either side of a dark central stripe.
Eyes:	Each of numerous black ocelli.
Lungs:	Two pairs.
Behaviour:	Initially remains motionless and is quite reluctant to move when prodded. When dislodged, it has a surprisingly fast turn of speed.
Preserved:	Yellow blotches fade after a few days, but the central dark stripe and the contrast between the dark head and lighter body remain obvious.

Habitat:	Walls and buildings, especially where these are built from limestone, or contain lime-rich mortar.
Distribution:	Widespread records from most parts of Britain and Ireland. It seems to be less common near to western coasts. Very common in drystone walls in the Cotswolds and mortared walls in north-east Scotland.
Comments:	*P. spinicornis* is often found at night crawling over walls and is fairly easy to spot with a torch. This is a most attractive species. *P. scaber* (common rough woodlouse) is sometimes covered with dull yellow blotches but these are never arranged in rows either side of a central broken dark stripe.

Porcellionides cingendus (= *Metoponorthus cingendus* of older literature) (PLATE 12A)

Maximum length:	7 mm
Colour in life:	Yellowish to reddish-brown mottled with dark grey. This species bears a superficial resemblance to *Philoscia muscorum* but is much more dull in appearance.
Eyes:	Each of numerous black ocelli.
Lungs:	Two pairs (*Philoscia muscorum* has none).
Behaviour:	Runs moderately fast when disturbed.
Preserved:	Body colour fades to cream-yellow but dark mottling remains.
Habitat:	Grassland, scrub or open woodland in grass tussocks or leaf litter.
Distribution:	A species which occurs mainly near the coasts of south-west Ireland, south and west England, and Wales. It has been found on Anglesey, in a garden in Liverpool and recently in a grazing marsh in North Essex, extending the known range shown in Harding and Sutton (1985).
Comments:	The 'dull' appearance and two pairs of lungs are good field characters for this species. The transverse ridge on each pereonite (Fig. 22a) is obvious in preserved specimens and this species is unlikely to be confused with any other British woodlouse.

Porcellionides pruinosus (= *Metoponorthus pruinosus* of older literature) (PLATE 12B)

Maximum length:	12 mm
Colour in life:	Purple-grey or orange with unique surface plum-like 'bloom' caused by the presence of millions of tiny spheres on the surface (Hadley and Hendricks, 1985). The white legs are prominent.
Eyes:	Each of numerous black ocelli.
Lungs:	Two pairs.
Behaviour:	Runs extremely fast and erratically when disturbed.
Preserved:	The 'bloom' vanishes and the colour fades slightly to grey-brown.
Habitat:	Almost all records for this species are from dungheaps. For obvious reasons, it is almost certainly under-recorded! It may also be abundant in compost heaps and around buildings where livestock are, or were once, kept. Also occurs under bark of decaying hardwood trees on pasture land.
Distribution:	Found in most parts of Britain and Ireland but is apparently more common in the east than in the west. Its preference for synanthropic habitats suggests that it is an old introduction to Britain which has become naturalised.
Comments:	This species is capable of very rapid population growth which probably explains its success at colonising disturbed sites with a concentration of animal

manure (Dangerfield and Telford, 1990). *P. pruinosus* is abundant throughout the 'organic' gardens at the Centre for Alternative Technology at Machynlleth in North Wales.

Stenophiloscia zosterae (= *Halophiloscia zosterae* of older literature)
(Fig. 16d)

Maximum length:	6 mm
Colour in life:	Sand with brownish mottling.
Eyes:	Each of numerous black ocelli.
Lungs:	None.
Behaviour:	I have not seen a live specimen of this species. However, the general form of preserved specimens suggests that the behaviour may be similar to that of *Halophiloscia couchi*.
Preserved:	Brownish mottling fades.
Habitat:	Shingle and shingle/mud beaches. This species is active at night—almost all specimens have been collected in pit-fall traps.
Distribution:	Very rare. It is known only from three sites in England on the coast of Devon, Norfolk and Essex. Despite extensive searching, this species has not been found since 1977. However, because of its habitat and the difficulty of collecting it in the field, *S. zosterae* is probably more common than current records would indicate. Thus, it has not been included in the Red Data Book of threatened species.
Comments:	A more comprehensive description of this species is given in Harding and Sutton (1985). However, the diagram of *S. zosterae* in this description does not closely resemble specimens collected from Slapton Ley in Devon that I have seen. Fig. 16d is based on these specimens rather than the diagram in Harding and Sutton (1985).

Trachelipus rathkei
(PLATE 11B)

Maximum length:	15 mm
Colour in life:	Dark grey mottled with orange and light grey patches, the latter arranged in parallel rows either side of the mid-line. It is never a uniform slate-grey colour. This species is superficially similar to a rather dark *Oniscus asellus*.
Eyes:	Each of numerous black ocelli.
Lungs:	Five pairs. Only one other species, *Cylisticus convexus* (PLATE 8B) also has five pairs of lungs.
Behaviour:	Initially remains motionless but runs quite fast when disturbed.
Preserved:	Orange pigmentation vanishes but the parallel rows of light patches remain.
Habitat:	Found in a wide range of habitats including rough grassland, marshland, rubbish tips, disused quarries etc.
Distribution:	Restricted to south-east England and the Midlands but within this area, may be locally common (Whitehead, 1988).
Comments:	The five pairs of lungs are an excellent field character which can be seen easily with the naked eye. Preserved specimens of *T. rathkei* look similar to *Porcellio spinicornis*. However, the rear margin of the head and first pereonite in *T. rathkei* are strongly curved (Fig. 21b) whereas in *P. spinicornis* they are almost straight.

Trichoniscoides albidus
(PLATE 5A)

Maximum length:	4 mm
Colour in life:	Reddish-brown with dull body surface contrasting with uropods and telson which are noticeably white. This species is often overlooked due to its similarity in size and colour to *Trichoniscus pusillus* which is much more common. However, *Trichoniscus pusillus* has a smooth dorsal surface whereas that of *Trichoniscoides albidus* is covered in rows of small bumps (compare PLATES 4A and 5A).
Eyes:	Each of a single large reddish-brown ocellus (Fig. 14b).
Lungs:	None.
Behaviour:	Moves slowly when disturbed (more like a *Haplophthalmus* than a *Trichoniscus*).
Preserved:	Fades gradually over a few days to off-white (hence specific name *albidus* = white). The colour of *Trichoniscus pusillus* does not fade in this way. The only certain way to distinguish preserved specimens of this species from the other three species of *Trichoniscoides*, and the two species of *Metatrichoniscoides*, is by comparing male first and second pleopods (Figs. 15a–f).
Habitat:	Wet sites under stones in natural and synanthropic sites (*e.g.* roadside ditches).
Distribution:	All records are from eastern, southern and central England and eastern Ireland, except for a population discovered at St. Bees in Cumbria in 1988.
Comments:	Most recorders, once they become familiar with this species, turn it up in the majority of 10 km squares in their area. Thus, *T. albidus* is almost certainly more widespread and common than current records would indicate.

Trichoniscoides helveticus
(general appearance as Fig. 7g)

Maximum length:	4 mm
Colour in life:	White flushed with pale pink (very similar to *Trichoniscoides sarsi* with which it has been confused in the past).
Eyes:	Each of one red ocellus (Fig. 14c).
Lungs:	None.
Behaviour:	Moves slowly when disturbed.
Preserved:	All pigments fade rapidly. The only certain way to distinguish preserved specimens of this species from the other three species of *Trichoniscoides*, and the two species of *Metatrichoniscoides*, is by comparing male first and second pleopods (Figs. 15a–f).
Habitat:	Soil-dwelling species found by turning over deeply-embedded boulders or digging. It seems to come to the surface after a heavy frost but past confusion with *T. sarsi* makes generalisation difficult.
Distribution:	The map showing records of *Trichoniscoides* 'sarsi' in Harding and Sutton (1985) contains records for both *T. sarsi* and *T. helveticus*. On present knowledge, *T. helveticus* occurs in south-east England and is probably a native species since it has been found in ancient woodlands. *T. sarsi* is only known from gardens or chuchyards in Dublin, Leicester and Kent and may be an old introduction.
Comments:	I discovered this species while examining male pleopods of specimens which had been identified as *T. sarsi*, based on the pink colouration and red ocelli.

This illustrates the importance of checking male pleopods of these small soil-dwelling species. *T. helveticus* is widespread in north-west Europe.

Trichoniscoides saeroeensis
(general appearance as Fig. 7g)

Maximum length:	4 mm
Colour in life:	White flushed with pale pink or orange (very similar to *Trichoniscoides helveticus* and *T. sarsi* with which it may have been confused in the past). In muddy sites, the body may be discoloured with particles of soil.
Eyes:	Each of one orange ocellus (Fig. 14c).
Lungs:	None.
Behaviour:	Moves slowly when disturbed.
Preserved:	All pigments fade rapidly. The only certain way to distinguish preserved specimens of this species from the other three species of *Trichoniscoides*, and the two species of *Metatrichoniscoides*, is by comparing male first and second pleopods (Figs. 15a–f).
Habitat:	Seashore only. Not recorded far above the splash zone. Found most easily by turning over stones at the base of eroding cliffs.
Distribution:	Known from about 70 sites around the coast of Britain and Ireland.
Comments:	This species is probably quite common and is certainly under-recorded. Male pleopods should be checked for definitive identification as occasionally, more pigmented specimens have turned up which appeared at first to be *T. albidus*.

Trichoniscoides sarsi
(general appearance as Fig. 7g)

Maximum length:	4 mm
Colour in life:	White flushed with pale pink (very similar to *Trichoniscoides helveticus* with which it has been confused in the past).
Eyes:	Each of one red ocellus (Fig. 14c).
Lungs:	None.
Behaviour:	Moves slowly when disturbed.
Preserved:	All pigments fade rapidly. The only certain way to distinguish preserved specimens of this species from the other three species of *Trichoniscoides*, and the two species of *Metatrichoniscoides*, is by comparing male first and second pleopods (Figs. 15a–f).
Habitat:	Soil-dwelling species found by turning over stones. It seems to come to the surface after a heavy frost but past confusion with *T. helveticus* makes generalisation difficult.
Distribution:	The map showing records of *Trichoniscoides* 'sarsi' in Harding and Sutton (1985) contains records for both *T. sarsi* and *T. helveticus*. On present knowledge, *T. sarsi* is only known from gardens or churchyards in Dublin, Leicester or Kent and may be an old introduction. *T. helveticus* occurs in South-east England and is probably a native species since it has been found in ancient woodlands.
Comments:	Specimens of *T. sarsi* cannot be definitely identified as such without checking male pleopods. It is possible that other species of *Trichoniscoides* may be 'hiding' in reference collections, waiting to be discovered by diligent isopodologists.

Trichoniscus pusillus (Common pygmy woodlouse)
(PLATE 4A)

Maximum length:	5 mm
Colour in life:	Reddish or purplish-brown. Occasionally, specimens are found infected with an iridovirus which gives the animal a vivid purple sheen (PLATE 4B). Yellow individuals also turn up but the cause of this colouration is not known.
Eyes:	Each of three black ocelli (Fig. 11).
Lungs:	None.
Behaviour:	Moves rapidly when disturbed.
Preserved:	Colour fades slightly but most body pigments remain. *T. pusillus* never fades to the white colour of *T. pygmaeus*.
Habitat:	Common in damp soil and leaf litter.
Distribution:	Very common and widespread throughout Britain and Ireland.
Comments:	*T. pusillus* is probably the most abundant woodlouse in woodland in Britain. In leaf litter it may reach densities of more than 500 per square metre (Phillipson, 1983). Populations of *T. pusillus* exist in two forms, *T. pusillus* form *pusillus* which is parthenogenetic and composed almost entirely of females, and *T. pusillus* form *provisorius* in which males and females occur in equal numbers. Separating the two forms on morphological grounds is extremely difficult and is outside the scope of this key. Further information on the two forms is given in Harding and Sutton (1985) and Fussey (1984).

Trichoniscus pygmaeus
(general appearance as Fig. 7e)

Maximum length:	2.5 mm
Colour in life:	Creamy white or white, sometimes with a pale pink flush rather similar to the colour of *Trichoniscoides helveticus* and *T. sarsi*. An apricot yellow specimen has been found on one occasion.
Eyes:	Each of three black ocelli arranged together in a tight group (Fig. 11).
Lungs:	None.
Behaviour:	Moves slowly when disturbed (more sluggish than *Trichoniscus pusillus*).
Preserved:	Fades to dead white with prominent black ocelli.
Habitat:	Damp soil and deep leaf litter.
Distribution:	Common and widespread and certainly under-recorded due to its small size.
Comments:	The male pleopods of this species are similar in appearance to *T. pusillus* and there is no clear morphological feature that can be used to separate the two species. However, *T. pygmaeus* is always less than 2.5 mm in length and is never pigmented to the same degree as *T. pusillus*. Even juvenile *T. pusillus* of less than 2.5 mm in length are more pigmented than *T. pygmaeus* so only the very small specimens are likely to cause identification problems. *T. pygmaeus* is a species worthy of detailed study as there may be other species 'hiding' under its name in the same manner as *Trichoniscoides* 'sarsi' and *Haplophthalmus* 'mengei'.

ACKNOWLEDGEMENTS

In writing the present work, I have drawn heavily on the earlier keys to woodlice written by Edney (1954) and Sutton, Harding and Burn (1972). These works stimulated research on woodlice which has led directly to the need for the present key. I am extremely grateful to fellow members of the British Isopod Study Group who have given freely of their time and advice, and have loaned or donated specimens which have helped in the preparation of this key. In particular I would like to thank Stephen Sutton, Arthur Chater, Adrian Rundle, Paul Lee, David Bilton, Andrew Roberts, Graham Oliver, George Fussey, Steve Gregory, Eric Philp, Douglas Richardson, Dave Guntrip, John Daws, David Holdich, Adrian Fowles, Charles Rawcliffe and Gordon Blower. Dr. H. Dalens, Dr. H. E. Gruner and Dr. H. Fechter kindly loaned specimens of *Haplophthalmus*. The revision of this genus in Britain and Ireland was made possible by a grant from the Omer-Cooper Bequest of the Linnean Society. Paul Harding at the Biological Records Centre has been a constant source of advice and encouragement for which I am most grateful. Finally, I would like to thank Steve Tilling for his help during the testing stage for this key and all the 'testers' whose comments greatly improved the finished version.

REFERENCES AND FURTHER READING

Sutton's (1972) book 'Woodlice' (which is still available) is the best general introduction to the group. Harding and Sutton's (1985) 'Woodlice in Britain and Ireland' contains a wealth of information on distribution. Harding (1990) includes an extensive list of references to earlier literature on woodlice. An up to date Linnean Society Synopsis of the British woodlice is being prepared; this will replace Edney's (1954) earlier version. European woodlice are covered in Vandel (1960, 1962) and Gruner (1966), but these publications were written for specialists (and those fluent in French and German!). The journal 'Isopoda' (published by the British Isopod Study Group) contains more general articles on woodlice and is available from the Isopod Scheme Organiser (address on page 604). The biology of terrestrial isopods from an international perspective has been reviewed by Warburg (1987).

The first two International Symposia on the 'Biology of Terrestrial Isopods' were held at the Zoological Society of London (7 to 8 July 1983), and Urbino, Italy (10 to 12 September 1986), and have been published as Sutton and Holdich (1984) and Ferrara (1989) respectively. They contain the most up to date information on the taxonomy, evolution, ecology and physiology of woodlice currently available, and are worth consulting if projects at the undergraduate level are being planned. More recently, Symposia on terrestrial isopods have been held at Poitiers, France (July 1990)and Godollo, Hungary (September 1991). The proceedings of these conferences should be published in the near future.

Publications quoted above and in the text are listed below.

BLINN, D. W., BLINN, S. L. and BAYLY, I. A. E. (1989). Feeding ecology of *Haloniscus searlei* Chilton, an oniscoid isopod living in Athalassic saline waters. *Australian Journal of Marine and Freshwater Research*, **40**, 295–301.

CHALMERS, N. and PARKER, P. (1989). *The OU Project Guide*. 2nd Ed. Occasional Publication of the Field Studies Council No. 9.

CHATER, A. O. (1988). Woodlice in the cultural consciousness of modern Europe. *Isopoda*, **2**, 21–39.

COLLOFF, M. J. and HOPKIN, S. P. (1986). The ecology, morphology and behaviour of *Bakerdania elliptica* (Acari: Prostigmata: Pygmephoridae), a mite associated with terrestrial isopods. *Journal of Zoology*, **208**, 109–123.

COLLOFF, M. J. and HOPKIN, S. P. (1987). Description of the adult male of *Bakerdania elliptica* (Krczal, 1959) with a redescription of the adult female (Acari: Pygmephoridae). *Acarologia*, **28**, 323–330.

DANGERFIELD, J. M. and TELFORD, S. R. (1990). Breeding phenology, variation in reproductive effort and offspring size in a tropical population of the woodlouse *Porcellionides pruinosus*. *Oecologia*, Berlin, **82**, 251–258.

EDNEY, E. B. (1954). *British Woodlice* (Synopses of the British Fauna, Old Series No. 9). London, Linnean Society.

FEDERICI, B. A. (1984). Diseases of terrestrial isopods. *Symposium of the Zoological Society of London*, **53**, 233–245.

FERRARA, F. ed. (1989). Proceedings of the Second Symposium on the Biology of Terrestrial Isopods. *Monitore Zoologico Italiano (New Series)*, *Monografia*, 4.

FUSSEY, G. D. (1984). The distribution of the two forms of the woodlouse *Trichoniscus pusillus* Brandt (Isopoda: Oniscoidea) in the British Isles : a reassessment of geographical parthenogenesis. *Biological Journal of the Linnean Society*, **22**, 309–321.

GRUNDY, A. J. and SUTTON, S. L. (1989). Year class splitting in the woodlouse *Philoscia muscorum* explained through studies of growth and survivorship. *Holarctic Ecology*, **12**, 112–119.

GRUNER, H. E. (1966). *Die Tierwelt Deutschlands:Krebstiere oder Crustacea. 5: Isopoda, vol. 2*. Jena, Fischer.

GUNNARSON, T. (1987). Selective feeding on a maple leaf by *Oniscus asellus* (Isopoda). *Pedobiologia*, **30**, 161–165.

HADLEY, N. F. and HENDRICKS, G. M. (1985). Cuticular microstructures and their relationship to structural colour and transpiration in the terrestrial isopod *Porcellionides pruinosus*. *Canadian Journal of Zoology*, **63**, 649–666

HAMES, C. A. C. (1987). Provisional atlas of the association between *Platyarthrus hoffmánnseggi* and ants in Britain and Ireland. *Isopoda*, **1**, 9–19.

HAMES, C. A. C. and HOPKIN, S. P. (1989). The structure and function of the digestive system of terrestrial isopods. *Journal of Zoology*, **217**, 599–627.

HASSALL, M. and RUSHTON, S. P. (1982). The role of coprophagy in the feeding strategies of terrestrial isopods. *Oecologia*, Berlin, **53**, 374–381.

HASSALL, M. and RUSHTON, S. P. (1985). The adaptive significance of coprophagous behaviour in the terrestrial isopod *Porcellio scaber*. *Pedobiologia*, **28**, 169–175.

HASSALL, M., TURNER, J. G. and RANDS, M. R. W. (1987). Effects of terrestrial isopods on the decomposition of woodland leaf litter. *Oecologia*, Berlin, **72**, 597–604.

HARDING, P. T. (1990). An indexed bibliography of the distribution and ecology of woodlice (Crustacea, Oniscidea) in Great Britain (1830–1986). *Isopoda*, **4**, 1–32.

HARDING, P. T. and SUTTON, S. L. (1985). *Woodlice in Britain and Ireland: Distribution and Habitat*. Huntingdon, Institute of Terrestrial Ecology.

HARDING, P. T. and SUTTON, S. L. (1988). The spread of the terrestrial amphipod *Arcitalitrus dorrieni* in Britain and Ireland : watch this niche! *Isopoda*, **2**, 7–10.

HAUG, T. and ALTNER, H. A. (1984). A cryofixation study of presumptive hygroreceptors on the antennule of a terrestrial isopod. *Tissue and Cell*, **16**, 377–392.

HOESE, B. (1984). The marsupium in terrestrial isopods. *Symposium of the Zoological Society, London*, **53**, 65–76.

HOESE, B. (1989). Morphological and comparative studies on the second antennae of terrestrial isopods. *Monitore Zoologica Italiano (New Series)*, *Monografia*, **4**, 127–152.

HOFFMANN, G. (1984). Orientation behaviour of the desert woodlouse *Hemilepistus reaumuri*: adaptations to ecological and physiological problems. *Symposium of the Zoological Society, London*, **53**, 405–422.

HOLDICH, C. M. (1984). The cuticular surface of woodlice: a search for receptors. *Symposium of the Zoological Society, London*, **53**, 9–48.

HOLDICH, D. M. LINCOLN, R. J. and ELLIS, J. P. (1984). The biology of terrestrial isopods: terminology and classification. *Symposium of the Zoological Society, London*, **53**, 1–6.

HOLT, V. M. (1885). *Why Not Eat Insects?* London, Field and Tuer (reprinted recently by E. W. Classey, PO Box 93, Faringdon, Oxon.).

HOPKIN, S. P. (1987). Biogeography of woodlice in Britain and Ireland. *Isopoda*, **1**, 21–36.

HOPKIN, S. P. (1988). The 'Reading Woodlouse Watch' 1987. *Isopoda*, **2**, 41–46.

HOPKIN, S. P. (1989a). *Ecophysiology of Metals in Terrestrial Invertebrates*. Elsevier Applied Science, Barking.

HOPKIN, S. P. (1989b). 'Albino' woodlice ; do they exist? *Isopoda*, **3**, 29–31.

HOPKIN, S. P. and ROBERTS, A. W. P. (1987). A species of *Haplophthalmus* new to Britain. *Isopoda*, **1**, 37–48.

HOPKIN, S. P., HARDISTY, G. N. and MARTIN, M. H. (1986). The woodlouse *Porcellio scaber* as a 'biological indicator' of zinc, cadmium, lead and copper pollution. *Environmental Pollution, Series B*, **11**, 271–290.

JONES, R. E. and PRATELY, P. (1987). Woodlice of the Isles of Scilly. *Isopoda*, **1**, 49–54.

JONES, S. P. (1987). A report on the woodlice of Cornwall. *Isopoda*, **1**, 55–64.

JONES-WALTERS, L. M. (1989). Keys to the families of British Spiders. *Field Studies*, **7**, 365–443.

MAIORANA, V. C. and VAN VALEN, L. M. (1985). Terrestrial isopods for preparing delicate vertebrate skeletons. *Systematic Zoology*, **34**, 242–245.

OLIVER, P. G. (1983). The occurrence of *Buddelundiella cataractae* Verhoeff, 1930 (Isopoda: Oniscoidea) in Wales, Great Britain. *Crustaceana*, **44**, 105–108.

OLIVER, P. G. and SUTTON, S. L. (1982). *Miktoniscus patiencei* Vandel, 1946 (Isopoda: Oniscoidea), a redescription with notes on its occurrence in Britain and Eire. *Journal of Natural History*, **16**, 201–208.

OLIVER, P. G. and TREW, A. (1981). A new species of *Metatrichoniscoides* (Crustacea: Isopoda: Oniscoidea) from the coast of South Wales, U.K. *Journal of Natural History*, **15**, 525–529.

PHILLIPSON, J. (1983). Life cycle, numbers, biomass and respiratory metabolism of *Trichoniscus pusillus* (Crustacea—Isopoda) in a beech woodland—Wytham Woods, Oxford. *Oecologia*, Berlin, **57**, 339–343.

PIEARCE, T. G. (1989). Acceptability of pteridophyte litters to *Lumbricus terrestris* and *Oniscus asellus* and implications for the nature of ancient soils. *Pedobiologia*, **33**, 91–100.

QUILTER, C. G. (1987). Foraging activity of the sand beach isopod *Scyphax ornatus* Dana. *New Zealand Journal of Zoology*, **14**, 433–439.

RICHARDSON, D. T. (1989). *Armadillidium pictum* Brandt in Yorkshire. *Isopoda*, **3**, 13–14.

SCHMALFUSS, H. (1984). Eco-morphological strategies in terrestrial isopods. *Symposium of the Zoological Society*, *London*, **53**, 49–63.

SEYMOUR, R. (1989). *Invertebrates of economic importance in Britain—common and scientific names*. London, HMSO.

SUNDERLAND, K. D. and SUTTON, S. L. (1980). A serological study of arthropod predation on woodlice in a dune grassland ecosystem. *Journal of Animal Ecology*, **49**, 987–1004.

SUTTON, S. L. (1972). *Woodlice*. London, Ginn (republished by Pergamon Press, Oxford, in 1980).

SUTTON, S. L. and HARDING, P. T. (1989). Interpretation of distribution of terrestrial isopods in the British Isles. *Monitore Zoologica Italiano (New Series)*, Monografia, **4**, 43–61.

SUTTON, S. L., HARDING, P. T. and BURN, D. (1972). *Key to British Woodlice*. pp. 81–104 in Sutton (1972).

SUTTON, S. L. and HOLDICH, D. M. Eds. (1984). *The Biology of Terrestrial Isopods* (Symposium of the Zoological Society of London no. 53). Oxford, Clarendon.

SUTTON, S. L. HASSALL, M., WILLOWS, R., DAVIS, R. C., GRUNDY, A. and SUNDERLAND, K. D. (1984). Life histories of terrestrial isopods: a study of intra- and interspecific variation. *Symposium of the Zoological Society, London*, **53**, 269–294.

THORNTON, M. (1989). The woodlouse sermon. *Isopoda*, **3**, 1–4.

TILLING, S. M. (1987). A key to the major groups of British terrestrial invertebrates. *Field Studies*, **6**, 695–766.

VADER, W. and DE WOLF, L. (1988). Biotope and biology of *Armadillium album* Dollfuss, a terrestrial isopod of sandy beaches, in the S.W. Netherlands. *Netherlands Journal of Sea Research*, **22**, 175–183.

VANDEL, A. (1960). *Isopodes Terrestres (Premiere Partie)*. Faune de France no. 64. Paris, Lechevalier.

VANDEL, A. (1962). *Isopodes Terrestres (Deuxieme Partie)*. Faune de France no. 66. Paris, Lechevalier.

WARBURG, M. R. (1987). Isopods and their terrestrial environment. *Advances in Ecological Research*, **17**, 187–242.

WHITEHEAD, P. F. (1988). New sites for *Trachelipus rathkei* in England. *Isopoda*, **2**, 11–14.

WILLIAMS, T. and FRANKS, N. R. (1988). Population size and growth rate, sex ratio and behaviour in the ant isopod *Platyarthrus hoffmannseggi*. *Journal of Zoology*, **215**, 703–717.

WILLMER, P. G., BAYLIS, M. and SIMPSON, C. L. (1989). The roles of colour change and behaviour in the hygrothermal balance of a littoral isopod, *Ligia oceanica*. *Oecologia*, Berlin, **78**, 349–356.

WRIGHT, J. C. and MACHIN, J. (1990). Water vapour absorption in terrestrial isopods. *Journal of Experimental Biology*, **154**, 13–30.

GLOSSARY

NOTE. Figures 2 and 3 are referred to extensively in the Glossary see p. 606 and 607.

ANTENNA (plural ANTENNAE): The pair of segmented structures ('feelers') which woodlice hold in front of the head while walking along (Fig. 2; see also FLAGELLUM and PEDUNCLE). All Crustacea have two pairs of antennae. In woodlice, it is the second (outermost) pair which are long and covered with sensory structures (Hoese, 1989). The first (innermost) pair have been much reduced in length during evolution and are extremely difficult to see in all species except the common sea slater *Ligia oceanica* and *Ligidium hypnorum*. Following the terminology of Holdich *et al.* (1984), the second pair are known as antennae and the tiny first pair as antennules. The antennules may be sensitive to humidity changes (Haug and Altner, 1984).

ANTERIOR: The front or 'head end' of woodlice.

BASIS: The first (innermost) segment of each leg (Fig. 3).

CARPUS: The fourth segment of each leg (counting from the innermost segment, the BASIS: Fig. 3).

COLOUR: The colours of woodlice are only used as main characters in the key when they do not fade significantly in preserved specimens. However, colour can be extremely useful when identifying living woodlice, so 'colour in life' is given in all the individual species accounts. Red, orange and most yellow pigments tend to fade completely in alcohol within a few hours whereas black, brown and grey pigments are much more permanent. In white woodlice, the contents of the gut often show through the cuticle as a central dark brown stripe. Some woodlice may be infected with a virus which gives them a purple sheen (seen most frequently in *Trichoniscus pusillus*—PLATE 4B). Much rarer are albino specimens of species which are normally heavily pigmented (Hopkin, 1989). These should key out to species in most cases but are unlikely to be encountered by the beginner (less than a dozen albinos have been found by contributors to the Isopod Survey Scheme in the past 20 years). They are most common in caves.

DACTYLUS: The outermost segment which forms the tip of each leg (Fig. 3).

DORSAL: The upper surface of woodlice. The 'smoothness' of the dorsal surface is quite an important character for identification and is used at several points in the key. The dorsal surface of all woodlice is covered with minute sensory structures called 'tricorns' because their appearance is similar to that of a three-cornered hat (Holdich, 1984). In addition, the cuticle may be formed into small bumps or ridges which are quite pronounced in the pygmy woodlice *Buddelundiella cataractae* (Fig. 7a) and *Haplophthalmus* sp. (Fig. 7b).

ENDOPOD(ITE): see UROPODS and PLEOPODS.

EPIMERA: the lateral edges of the PEREON and PLEON (Figs. 2, 3).

EXOPOD(ITE): see UROPODS and PLEOPODS.

EYES: see OCELLUS.

FLAGELLUM (plural FLAGELLA): The segments at the end of each antenna separated from the PEDUNCLE by a distinct 'bend' (Fig. 2). The number of segments in the flagellum is an extremely important character (Fig. 5). The surface of the flagellum is covered with tiny sensory structures which provide information on humidity, taste and texture. As woodlice walk along, they tap the flagella against the ground, or wave them in the air, to obtain information on their surroundings (Hoese, 1989). During evolution, the number of segments in the flagellum has been reduced. In the most 'primitive' species such as *Ligia oceanica* (PLATE 1B), the flagellum contains numerous segments. In pygmy woodlice (family Trichoniscidae), the flagellum actually contains six segments but these have fused together so the structure appears to consist of only one distinct conical section (and is referred to as such in the key). The joins between these segments are only visible under high magnification in a light microscope, or in a scanning electron microscope. The next most 'advanced' species such as the common shiny woodlouse *Oniscus asellus* (PLATE 7A) have three segments to the flagellum, and the most advanced, such as *Porcellio spinicornis*, have two segments (PLATE 9B). The number of distinct sections to the flagellum of all British species are given in the checklist on page 605.

IRIDOVIRUS: A virus infection of woodlice which gives them a distinct purple 'sheen' (PLATE 4B) (Federici, 1984).

ISCHIUM: The second segment of each leg (counting from the innermost segment, the BASIS: Fig. 3).

LEG: see PEREOPOD.

LENGTH: The length is measured from the front of the head to the tip of the telson (Fig. 2). Some preservatives may 'relax' specimens making them slightly longer than when alive.

LUNGS: see PLEOPODAL LUNGS.

MANCA: All woodlice have six pairs of legs when released from the brood pouch of the female. At this stage they are called mancas. After the first moult, which occurs within 24 hours of release, the 7th leg-bearing segment appears and after another moult they gain their full complement of legs and are juveniles (Holdich *et al.*, 1984).

MERUS: The third segment of each leg (counting from the innermost segment, the BASIS: Fig. 3).

OCELLUS (plural OCELLI): An ocellus is the structure consisting of a single lens which woodlice use to detect light and dark. In British and Irish woodlice which are not blind, the eyes may each contain one, three or numerous (more than eight) ocelli. The ocelli of most species contain black pigments which do not fade in alcohol. However, in the genus *Trichoniscoides*, the single ocellus in each eye is reddish-brown, orange or red. Unfortunately, the precise shade is variable and the pigments fade in alcohol. Thus, the colour of the ocelli cannot be used as a definitive character for the identification of preserved specimens of this genus. In woodlice with black eye pigments, the number of ocelli in each eye is important and is used extensively in the key. *Ligia oceanica* (PLATE 1B) has the largest eyes with several hundred ocelli.

PARTHENOGENETIC: A parthenogenetic population contains females which are able to produce offspring without mating with a male. Females of *Trichoniscus pusillus* are definitely able to do this. Other species, such as *Porcellio dilatatus*, may be parthenogenetic also.

PEDUNCLE: The five basal segments of each antenna separated from the FLAGELLUM by a distinct 'bend' (Fig. 2).

PEREON: The anterior (front) part of a woodlouse consisting of seven segments (the PEREONITES: Fig. 2), each of which bears a pair of walking legs (the PEREOPODS). The pereon and PLEON may be difficult to recognise as being separate parts of the body in some species (*e.g.* Fig. 18a) whereas in others (*e.g.* 18b) the distinction is obvious. Species with a clearly separate pereon and pleon tend to be much more 'sprightly' woodlice with a faster turn of speed (Schmallfuss, 1984). Those species without this clear junction are more prone to clinging to the substratum (*e.g.* PLATE 6A), or are able to roll into a ball (*e.g.* PLATE 14B).

PEREONITES: see PEREON.

PEREOPOD: The leg of a woodlouse. Apart from very young woodlice which have six pairs of legs (see MANCAS), all juvenile and adult woodlice have seven pairs (see also PEREON). When woodlice mate, the male climbs on to the back of the female and maintains his position by grasping her body with his legs. The arrangement of spines and shape of the seventh (last) pair of legs of male woodlice has evolved in response to this behaviour and in many cases, is unique to particular species. Thus, males of some species pairs, which may be difficult to separate using other characters, can be identified by examining these legs (*e.g. Haplophthalmus mengei* and *H. montivagus*—Fig. 9b, c).

PLEON: The posterior (rear) part of a woodlouse consisting of five segments (the PLEONITES: Fig. 2), each of which bears a set of paired plates (the PLEOPODS) on the ventral surface (Fig. 3).

PLEOPODAL LUNGS: The cuticle of the pleopods of woodlice is extremely thin. It is thought that the moist surfaces of these structures are the main sites of exchange of oxygen, carbon dioxide and water vapour (Wright and Machin, 1990). In some or all of the pleopods of the more 'advanced' species, the surface area available for gaseous exchange is increased substantially by the presence of numerous small internal channels. The channels open directly to the air via a small pore on each pleopod. These structures are known as pleopodal lungs (Holdich *et al.*, 1984) because the gas exchange is between the air and the blood (as in the lungs of humans). Each lung appears as a conspicuous white patch which can be seen easily with the naked eye. British and Irish woodlice which possess lungs may have either two or five (PLATE 8B) pairs (see Checklist p. 605). Lungs cannot be seen once a specimen has been immersed in alcohol.

PLEOPODS: Five sets of paired plates on the ventral surface of the PLEON (Fig. 3). Each pleopod consists of two parts, the ENDOPODITE, and the overlying EXOPODITE. In male woodlice, the first and second pleopods are modified to aid transfer of sperm to the female during mating (Fig. 3). Their structure in males is very important for the identification of some species (*e.g.* Fig. 15). The pleopods of some species are modified to form lungs (see PLEOPODAL LUNGS).

POSTERIOR: The rear or 'tail end' of woodlice.

PROPODUS: The fifth segment of each leg (counting from the innermost segment, the BASIS: Fig. 3).

SCUTELLUM: A structure on the 'forehead' of pill woodlice (*Armadillidium* sp.—Fig. 25g–l). The shape of the scutellum, and the extent of the ridge which forms its dorsal edge, are useful in identification.

SYNANTHROPIC: Associated with human activity. Synanthropic sites include buildings, walls, rubbish tips, gardens etc.

TELSON: The 'tail' of woodlice at the posterior end (Fig. 2).

TUBERCLES: Small raised bumps on the dorsal surface of some species of woodlice (most obvious in *Porcellio scaber*—PLATE 11A, Fig. 21a).

UROPODS: A pair of 'spear-shaped' (Fig. 4b), pointed (Fig. 4c) or 'spadelike' (Fig. 4a) structures on each side of the TELSON at the posterior end of woodlice. Each uropod is composed of two parts, the ENDOPODITE and the EXOPODITE (Figs. 2 and 3). Species with long and tubular uropods use them to remove excess water (*e.g.* a raindrop) from the body. The uropods are held together to form a capillary channel down which water is lost on to the ground (PLATE 3B). This can be demonstrated easily in *Oniscus asellus* or *Porcellio scaber*, by submerging them briefly in tap water, and then allowing the woodlice to walk over absorbent paper. They will repeatedly press their uropods against the paper until all the excess water has been lost. Addition of a drop of ink to the water will provide a permanent record and seems to do the woodlice no harm.

VENTRAL: The underside of woodlice.

The **AIDGAP** Project

The accurate identification of specimens is a fundamental part of most forms of biological fieldwork. Although the "popular" groups, such as butterflies, moths, birds and wild flowers, are well-served by numerous aids to identification, other groups are often neglected. The principal objectives of the AIDGAP project are to identify those groups for which the difficulty in identification is due to the absence of a simple and accurate key rather than being due to insuperable taxonomic problems and, subsequently, to produce simple, well-written aids to identification. These aids avoid obscure terminology, are clearly illustrated and need not be restricted to traditional methods of presentation. For example, the AIDGAP keys to willows and grasses have used multi-access tabular and punched-card formats.

The Field Studies Council is grateful to the British Ecological Society and Linnean Society of London for support during the testing and production of AIDGAP guides.

A significant feature of all the keys is the extent to which they are "tested" before final publication. In addition to routine editing and refereeing by acknowledged experts, the keys are subjected to extensive field tests. Several hundred copies of a preliminary draft – the "test" version – are sent to potential users: school and university staff; students; amateur naturalists; research workers; and others involved in surveys who need to identify organisms in groups outside their own sphere of interest. The authors are asked to amend the keys in the light of feedback from these "testers" before final publication.

LINNEAN SOCIETY OF LONDON

British Ecological Society

The success of any project such as this depends on feedback from the public. Most people who have experience of fieldwork are aware of "gaps" in the literature but unless these are communicated to the project co-ordinator, AIDGAP can do little to help alleviate the situation. Anyone wishing to contribute identification aids, or to suggest possible subjects for future projects, should contact the co-ordinator at the address alongside. Projects need not be confined to the biological field; AIDGAP would be equally interested in geological, palaeontological and geographical subjects.

AIDGAP
AIDS TO IDENTIFICATION
IN DIFFICULT GROUPS OF
ANIMALS & PLANTS

Field Studies Council
Preston Montford, Shrewsbury
Shropshire SY4 1HW

Telephone: 01743 852140
Fax: 01743 852101

e-mail:
publications@field-studies-council.org
www.field-studies-council.org

NOTES

NOTES

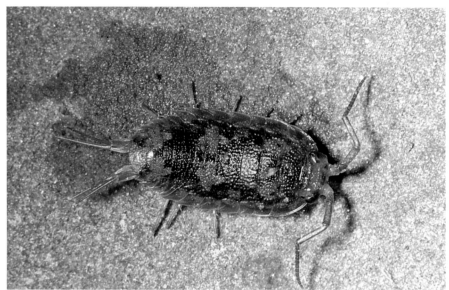

PLATE 1A
Ligia oceanica (common sea slater) of 25 mm in length. This species is widespread and common on rocky shores around the entire coast of Britain and Ireland.

PLATE 1B
Head and left antenna of *Ligia oceanica*. The flagellum of the antenna is composed of numerous distinct sections and the large black eyes composed of several hundred ocelli cover the side of the head (compare with Fig. 5a).

PLATE 2A

Haplophthalmus montivagus of 3 mm in length. Note the projections on the third pleonite (arrow) which are present also in *Haplophthalmus mengei*, but not in *Haplophthalmus danicus* (compare with Figs. 9a–c).

PLATE 2B

Metatrichoniscoides leydigi of 4 mm in length (right) and *Haplophthalmus mengei* (left). The dorsal sculpturing of *M. leydigi* consists of transverse rows of bumps whereas *H. mengei* is ornamented with pronounced longitudinal ridges (compare with Figs. 7b, 7g).

PLATE 3A
Oritoniscus flavus of 7 mm in length. This is an extremely fast-running species which has only been found in S.E. Ireland.

PLATE 3B
Androniscus dentiger (rosy woodlouse) of 6 mm in length, one of the most attractively coloured of all British woodlice. This specimen is getting rid of excess water. The drop will eventually be deposited on the substrate via the uropods which are held together to form a capillary channel.

PLATE 4A
Trichoniscus pusillus (common pygmy woodlouse) of 5 mm in length. This is the most abundant species of woodlouse in woodland leaf litter and is found throughout the British Isles.

PLATE 4B
Trichoniscus pusillus of 4 mm in length infected with an iridovirus which gives the animal a purple 'sheen'.

PLATE 5A
Trichoniscoides albidus of 3 mm in length. Note the transverse rows of small bumps on the pereonites (compare with Fig. 7g).

PLATE 5B
Platyarthrus hoffmannseggi (ant woodlouse) of 3 mm in length. This species is always found associated with ants, usually in their nests.

PLATE 6A
Oniscus asellus (common shiny woodlouse) The specimen on the left (of 10 mm in length) is the typical colour form whereas the form on the right is the scarce orange variety.

PLATE 6B
Philoscia muscorum (common striped woodlouse). The largest specimen is of 9 mm in length. Note the variation in colouration between individuals. Yellow forms are often found, especially near the sea.

PLATE 7A
Oniscus asellus (common shiny woodlouse) of 12 mm in length viewed from the left side. The antennal flagellum has three distinct sections and the eyes are composed of about 25 ocelli.

PLATE 7B
Halophiloscia couchi of 7 mm in length. The extremely long antennae are a characteristic feature of this species which is restricted to the coast. Note that the antennal flagellum is of three distinct sections.

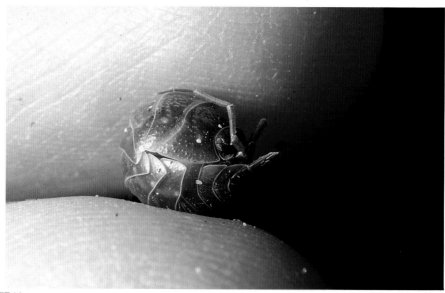

PLATE 8A

Cylisticus convexus of 13 mm in length in its characteristic posture with the antennae folded over the dorsal surface and prominent uropods and telson projecting outwards (compare with Fig. 19a).

PLATE 8B

Ventral view of *Cylisticus convexus* of 13 mm in length showing the five pairs of pleopodal lungs (white patches). The only other British species to have five pairs of lungs is *Trachelipus rathkei* (PLATE 11B).

PLATE 9A
Porcellio laevis of 15 mm in length. This species has a very smooth dorsal surface which gives it a glossy appearance.

PLATE 9B
Porcellio spinicornis of 12 mm in length. The head of this species is always black in contrast to the rest of the body which usually bears a row of bright yellow blotches either side of a central broken dark stripe (compare with Fig. 20c). Note that the antennal flagellum is of two distinct sections.

PLATE 10A
Porcellio dilatatus of 15 mm in length. Adults of this species are much wider in comparison to their length than the other *Porcellio* species.

PLATE 10B
Uropods and *telson* of *Porcellio dilatatus*. The rounded tip to the telson is a characteristic feature of this species.

PLATE 11A
Porcellio scaber (common rough woodlouse) of 11 mm in length, being attacked by the woodlouse-eating spider *Dysdera crocata*.

PLATE 11B
Trachelipus rathkei of 10 mm in length. This species has five pairs of pleopodal lungs on the ventral side which can be seen easily with the naked eye. The only other British species with five pairs of lungs is *Cylisticus convexus* (PLATE 8B).

PLATE 12A
Porcellionides cingendus of 7 mm in length. Note the transverse ridge on each segment of the pereon and the clear distinction between the pereon (anterior) and pleon (posterior) sections of the body (compare with Fig. 22a). The antennal flagellum is of two distinct sections.

PLATE 12B
Porcellionides pruinosus. The specimen on the extreme left is of 9 mm in length. Note the surface 'bloom' which gives these woodlice a 'plum-like' appearance in the field.

PLATE 13A
Eluma purpurascens of 8 mm in length. The surface of the body is covered with tiny 'hairs' and each eye is composed of a single large ocellus.

PLATE 13B
Armadillidium album of 6 mm in length. The surface of the body is covered with tiny spines and each eye is composed of several ocelli. This species is restricted to the coast.

PLATE 14A

Armadillidium pulchellum of 4 mm in length. This is a tiny species which when rolled up has a diameter of less than 2 mm. The posterior edge of the first pereonite is chamfered, a characteristic feature which separates *A. pulchellum* from the other pill woodlice (compare with Fig. 25d).

PLATE 14B

Armadillidium pictum of 7 mm in length, rolled into a ball with a diameter of about 3 mm. This is the rarest British woodlouse and is the only species (apart from the common pill woodlouse *Armadillidium vulgare*, PLATE 16A) able to roll into a perfect sphere.

PLATE 15A
Armadillidium depressum of 16 mm in length. Note the 'tortoise-like' appearance of the edges of the pereonites and pleonites which splay out like a skirt (see Fig. 25n).

PLATE 15B
Armadillidium depressum, the same specimen as in PLATE 15A but viewed from the left side showing animal rolled into a ball. This species always leaves an opening in contrast to *Armadillidium vulgare* (common pill woodlouse) which forms a completely sealed ball (Plate 16).

PLATE 16A
Armadillidium vulgare (common pill woodlouse) of 12 mm in length (left) rolled into a ball with a diameter of about 5 mm. This species is sometimes confused with the pill millipede *Glomeris marginata* (right). However, the ball formed by *G. marginata* is irregular in comparison to the much more spherical pill woodlice.

PLATE 16B
Armadillidium vulgare (common pill woodlouse). The rolled up specimen on the left is the typical colour form whereas that on the right (of 12 mm in length) is the less common pink variety.